Great Rooms!
How to Organize Your Classroom for Effective Learning

Grades 2–3

By
Michelle Thompson

Published by Frank Schaffer Publications
an imprint of

 Children's Publishing

Author: Michelle Thompson
Editor: Sara Freeman

Children's Publishing

Published by Frank Schaffer Publications
An imprint of McGraw-Hill Children's Publishing
Copyright © 2004 McGraw-Hill Children's Publishing

Send all inquiries to:
McGraw-Hill Children's Publishing
3195 Wilson Drive NW
Grand Rapids, Michigan 49544

Great Rooms! How to Organize Your Classroom for Effective Learning—grades 2–3
ISBN: 0-7682-2608-2

1 2 3 4 5 6 7 8 9 MAL 09 08 07 06 05 04

Table of Contents

Introduction

Great Rooms! How to Organize Your Classroom for Effective Learning gives you valuable insights and practical tips that will save you time and effort as you work towards producing a stimulating learning environment. When you are prepared and organized, the everyday tasks of teaching become easier, classroom management is achieved with confidence, and you are left with more time and energy to do what you love to do best—teach children.

This book includes information that pertains to classroom setup and seating arrangements, sections on effective discipline techniques, and important strategies for positive communications. Creative ideas abound for instilling a bright and welcoming classroom with eye-catching displays that engage and interest learners. There are useful lists for substitute teacher preparation, special events and field trips, learning center projects and preparations, and volunteers in the classroom.

Establishing a warm and open environment starts even before your students enter the classroom for the first time. Setting up your classroom for maximum learning builds a sense of safety where students will feel that they are free to learn, experiment, and grow as life-long learners.

You will find that you will have more time for one-on-one conferences, small group remediation or whole class enrichment, once the tools are set in place to maximize "up" time for effective learning. The routines, interactive decoratives, schedules, forms and letters are effective vehicles for communication, which is the first step in building a sense of community beyond the physical environment of the classroom.

Positive reinforcement ideas, self-esteem incentives, awards, engaging learning centers, realistic grade expectations, and a sense of order, set the stage for a smooth and productive learning environment.

If working smarter—not harder—is your goal, the strategies in *Great Rooms! How to Organize Your Classroom for Effective Learning* will become your essential resource for creating a vibrant and effective environment with a strong sense of community built on trust, fairness, and the necessary skills invaluable for effective learning.

You will need to decide where to put your desk. Do you want to place it near the doorway or the front of the room where students can easily see it? Either location is a good choice if you like to greet students from your desk as they enter the room each morning. Placing your desk in a clearly visible spot is useful if you like to sit at your desk when the class is working independently. From your desk, you can quickly gaze across the room to see if a student is having trouble staying on task or is having problems with work. On the other hand, you may prefer to place your desk in a quiet, far-off corner of the classroom. This arrangement is especially helpful if you plan to use your desk for individual conferences with students.

There are some teachers who use their desks solely for organizational purposes and as a staging area for lessons. Most record keeping is done at the computer when students are not in the classroom. If you will teach standing at the front of the room and like to walk to groups of students while presenting lessons or assignments, you may want to move your desk to the side of the room, in front, close to the chalkboard or whiteboard. You may also want to invest in a tall wooden stool to place in the front of the room to sit on when reading aloud, giving directions, or greeting the class at the beginning of the day.

Chapter 1: Classroom Environment

The organization and look of your classroom sets the tone for the learning environment that you create for the children in your class. Just as the interior design of a home tells visitors about the lifestyle of its inhabitants, the arrangement and setup of your classroom communicates volumes to students and parents about what to expect. How you arrange your classroom is a personal choice that is entirely up to you. The clever ideas and tips in this chapter will highlight a variety of available options.

Read this chapter to find out about:

- arranging students' desks
- organizing your teacher desk
- bulletin board displays
- chalkboards and whiteboards
- supplies and storage
- classroom library
- lost and found

Arranging Students' Desks

Depending on the amount of space you have to work with, there are a variety of different and effective ways to arrange the students' desks in your classroom. It is important to be sure that the desks are arranged so that all eyes can be fixed on you when you are addressing the class. Having the ability to connect eye-to-eye with each student will reduce behavior problems and allow you to easily check for comprehension during instruction.

Before selecting an appropriate seating arrangement for your classroom, there are a few factors that are important to consider:

- Doorways and high-traffic walkways should be kept clear for safety reasons. Make sure that doors and windows are accessible to students in case the need arises to make an emergency exit.

- Students with special needs may require wheelchair access or an area with limited visual distractions. Finding out about these needs prior to arranging your classroom will be helpful in selecting an appropriate setup.

- The type of seating you choose largely depends on the type of instruction you intend to use. For instance, if your students do most of their work individually, you may want to limit the amount of contact they have with other students while they are sitting in their seats. However, if cooperative learning is a focus for your classroom, you may want to organize the desks into clusters.

0-7682-2608-2 *Great Rooms! Grades 2–3*

Arranging Students' Desks

Rows and Rows and Rows

Some teachers choose to organize their students' desks in rows so that all desks are separated and students squarely face the front of the room. These rows create clean lines and an orderly feel to the room. This arrangement is beneficial for test-taking, independent seat work, and listening to lectures. However, it is not the most efficient for facilitating whole-class discussions or group work, as it limits the amount of contact students have with one another. When using this desk arrangement, it is helpful to carefully assign seats so that students who require additional attention, assistance, or monitoring are seated at the front of the classroom.

Two by Two

Arranging desks in pairs with an aisle separating each row is a great way to save a few inches of space while providing students with a learning partner. This setup allows all students to squarely face the front of the classroom, yet provides them with instant learning buddies. When using this arrangement, you may want to consider seating students with differing abilities next to one another so that one can serve as a model for the other. This arrangement also has the added benefit of creating easy transitions for cooperative learning. To make a group of four, students need only to turn around to work with the pair behind them.

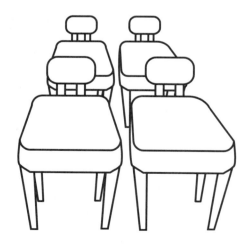

Arranging Students' Desks

Cluster Seating

Arranging desks in clusters of four lends itself to a more collaborative working environment for the students. This arrangement is an effective practice when you know your students will be engaged in many group activities. When arranging the group of four, try having the front two desks face each other and the back two desks sit side-by-side. Be sure to angle the desks so that each student has a clear, unobstructed view of the front of the classroom.

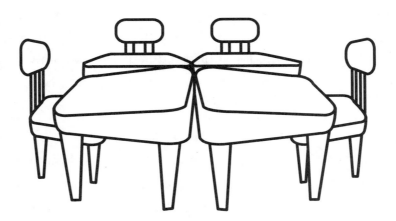

U-Shaped Arrangement

The U-shaped arrangement works well for classroom discussions or demonstrations. It connects students' desks and surrounds the central space of the room, allowing students to have a clear view of the entire room and each other. Ideally, the open part of the U should be at the front of the classroom. This allows all students to see the front of the classroom by either facing forward or simply turning their heads. This arrangement is also a good choice if space is needed for writing tables or learning centers in the middle of the room.

0-7682-2608-2 *Great Rooms!* Grades 2–3

Organizing Your Teacher Desk

Keeping your teaching materials organized and at your fingertips is essential to running a smooth classroom. Having a clear and orderly workspace will also help set the tone for organization and management of your classroom environment. Placing too many items on your desk can become visually distracting, so give some thought to the items that are must-haves. Add a personal touch such as a small plant or framed photograph if you desire.

Teacher Supplies

Keep your desk drawers well stocked with grading pens, pencils, paper clips, tape, chalk or markers, and extra erasers. It is also handy to have a pair of scissors, a stapler, and a bottle of glue reserved only for your use. Placing these items in drawers will keep your desktop free of clutter and reduce students' temptation to borrow school supplies from your desk.

Lesson Plans

Select a lesson plan book that suits your needs and use it to schedule and plan your lessons in detail week by week. For easy access, open your lesson plan book to the appropriate week and place it in the center of your desk. Giving your plan book this prime location will allow you to review your plans at a glance, make notes in the margins for future adjustments, and serve as a scheduling reminder for yourself. Also, in case of your absence, this obvious positioning allows a substitute to easily find your plans and continue with your lessons for the day.

0-7682-2608-2 *Great Rooms! Grades 2–3*

Papers

Grade Book

Many schools require that teachers keep their grade books on a computer file; however, if you still maintain a paper version of your grade book, be sure to keep it safely tucked away in a drawer of your desk or locked in a file cabinet. While it may seem handy to keep your grade book out and available, maintaining student confidentiality is important—so your grade book should not be accessible for others to see.

Student Papers

You may want to place a tray on your desk to hold student papers that are to be used with your lessons each day. One effective method of organizing these papers is by using five different-colored folders for each day of the week. At the beginning of the week, photocopy and sort the papers into the appropriate day's folder and store the folders in the tray, ready to be used.

Office Papers

As most primary teachers know, handling administrative paperwork can take a large amount of time unless you are organized. To reduce the amount of time spent sorting and collecting papers that are to be shuttled to and from the office, set up a tray or basket marked "Office" and place it on your desk. Every morning, have students place notes or forms that are to be sent to the office in the tray. Once these papers are collected, place them in an envelope and have a student helper make a trip to the office to deliver the papers at one time.

Teachers' Editions

Most school-adopted curriculums come complete with Teachers' Editions for each book. Because these books are usually large and require additional space, you may want to position a bookshelf or file cabinet behind or near your desk in which you can store them. As with most teacher supplies, it is important to have these books at your fingertips and ready to use as you make the transition from one subject to the next.

0-7682-2608-2 *Great Rooms! Grades 2–3*

Bulletin Board Displays

Creating colorful, decorative bulletin board displays is an effective way to welcome students to their new classroom and set a positive tone for the school year. Especially in primary grades, children love to see their names in print and their own artful creations on display.

Colorful sheets of butcher paper make ideal backgrounds, but don't be afraid to experiment with other materials and textures, such as wrapping paper, fabric, newspaper, or corrugated cardboard. Add commercial trimmers for borders, or create three-dimensional borders from wired ribbon or garland. The more creative you are, the more your bulletin boards will add to the festivity of your classroom.

The following pages contain suggestions for esteem-building slogans and displays that will help you set expectations for success in your classroom. You will also find reproducible patterns on pages 16-19 that you may want to use to recreate these ideas for your own bulletin boards.

Our Class Is Tee-riffic!

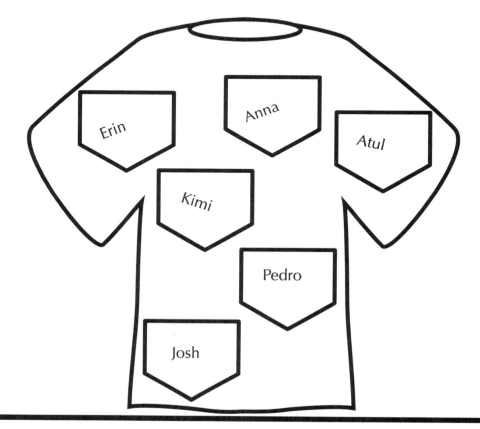

Bulletin Board Displays

What a Great Bunch of Second Graders!

This Year Will Be a Bushel of Fun!

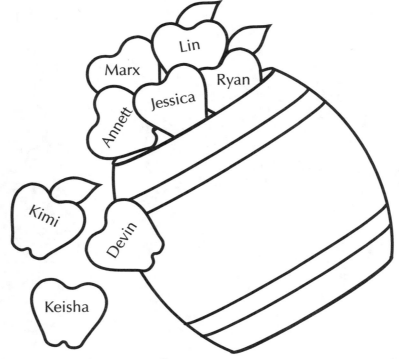

0-7682-2608-2 *Great Rooms! Grades 2–3*

Bulletin Board Displays

Step Into Success!

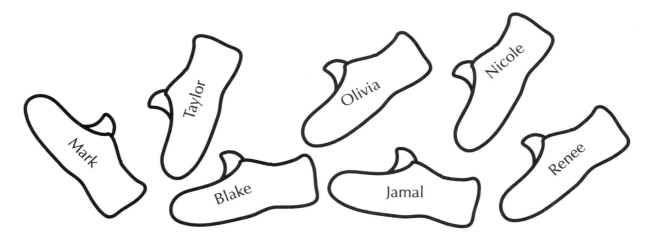

Let's Leap Into Learning!

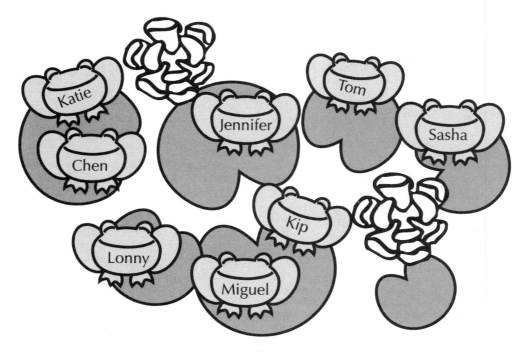

14

Our School Is Oceans of Fun!

Tip: To create easy coral reef seaweed, twist brightly colored crepe paper into spirals and staple the ends at the top and bottom of the bulletin board. Add a little pizzaz by hot gluing flat glass marbles (found at most craft stores) to create shimmering bubbles.

T-Shirt and Grape Leaf Patterns

Apple and Sneaker

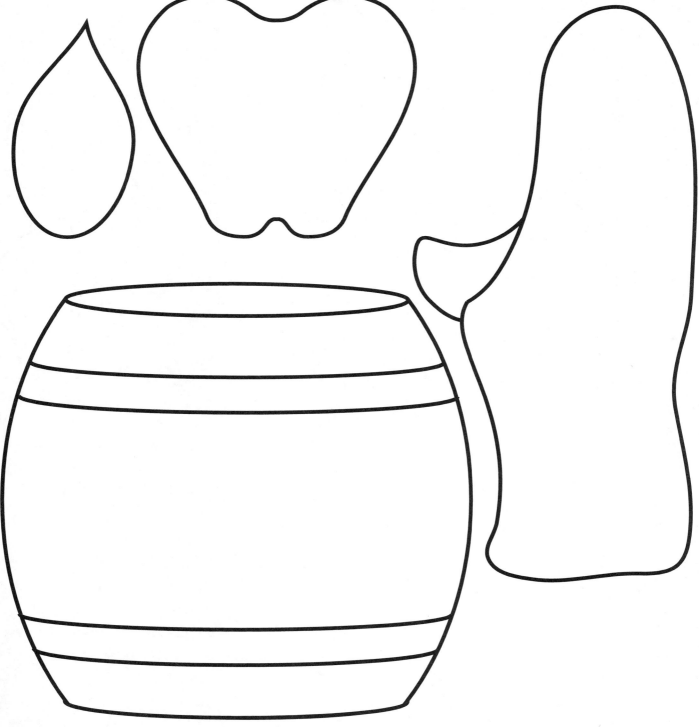

Frog and Lily Pads

Tip: To make a water lily, three petal patterns are needed for each flower. Cut the patterns out and line them up by pushing a pin through their centers. Next, splay the petals to form a daisy and curl them inward by gently rolling them with a pencil. Curl the top layer of petals tightest and staple or pin the water lily directly to the board.

Bulletin Board Patterns

Tropical Fish

Angelfish

Bannerfish

Butterflyfish

0-7682-2608-2 *Great Rooms! Grades 2–3*

Chalkboards and Whiteboards

If you plan to utilize chalkboards or whiteboards for a majority of your instruction, be sure that they are positioned in a location that is easy for all students to see. If your chalkboards or whiteboards are stationary and cannot be moved, take care to position students' desks so that they are facing the boards.

Chalkboard or Whiteboard?

Due to some children's allergies to chalk dust, many schools choose to supply their classrooms with whiteboards instead of chalkboards. If you are starting the year in a new school or classroom, you may want to find out in advance whether your room will have chalkboards or whiteboards. Once you know which type of board you will be using, attain the appropriate writing utensils for the board (chalk or markers).

Welcoming Your Students

On the first day of school, write a message on the board to welcome students into your classroom. Printing a simple phrase such as *Welcome to Second Grade! My name is Mrs. Johnson.* is likely to help reassure nervous students that they are in the correct classroom. You may also want to write simple directions on the board for a short assignment so that students will be introduced to your morning routine from the first minute they set foot in your classroom. This is a great way to start the morning and set positive expectations for your students.

Chalkboards and Whiteboards

Chalk or Marker Storage

It is easy to lose whiteboard markers or small pieces of chalk. To organize your markers or chalk and your erasers, set a small plastic bowl or cardboard shoebox on a stool next to the board in which supplies may be stored. Or, purchase an inexpensive cosmetic hanging bag and hang it on a hook next to the board. Fill the little compartments with different-colored markers or chalk and erasers.

Using Boards During Lessons

When setting up your classroom, be sure to leave room for you to stand on either side of the chalkboard without obstructing the view of the board for students. While writing on the board during lessons, you will want to angle your body so that your back is never completely turned to the students. This will help you visually check if students are attentive and if they are having any problems understanding what you are writing. It also sends a message to your students that you are always aware of what is taking place in the room.

Student Boards

You may want to purchase a class set of small wipe boards or chalk slates for students to use at their desks. This will allow you to engage all students in lessons by having them write on the boards without leaving their seats. Students will enjoy this unique form of participation, and it will help you determine at a glance whether students are mastering concepts or need further explanation and instruction.

Supplies and Storage

A large part of organizing your classroom involves finding a place to store a variety of classroom essentials, such as students' belongings, art supplies, paper goods, portfolios, and more! Even classrooms with the most challenging spaces can be organized by using a few creative storage ideas.

Lunch Boxes

Many students will have lunch boxes or lunch bags that they carry with them to school. Some schools provide each classroom with a large plastic tub for storing and transporting lunches. If yours does not, you will want to set up an area of the room where students can store their items until lunchtime. A bookshelf or cubbies attached to the wall for each student work well. If space is limited, attach stick-on plastic hooks to the side or bottom of students' desks and have students hang their lunch bags from their desks. Whichever way you choose, you will want to keep the lunch boxes off the ground so they will not be trampled, but within reach of the students so they do not need your assistance in retrieving and storing their lunches each day.

Backpacks

Student backpacks require a large amount of space. Depending on your school building and climate, you may want to have students leave backpacks outside the classroom in lockers or cubbies that you can easily purchase or build yourself from plywood. If weather or your school setup does not permit this arrangement, attach sturdy metal hooks about four inches apart to strips of two-by-fours and mount them horizontally on a wall in your classroom, one board on top of the other, about eight inches apart. Have students hang their backpacks on a designated hook each morning. This will keep them out of the way and prevent the creation of a huge and messy backpack pile!

Hats and Coats

The metal hooks described for the backpacks above will work for hats and coats as well. Or, if limited wall space does not permit you to use this arrangement, purchase an inexpensive freestanding coat rack to place in a corner of the room. If this is not a possibility, simply have students drape their coats over the backs of their chairs to keep them out of the way during class time.

0-7682-2608-2 Great Rooms! Grades 2–3

Student Supplies

You may want to provide students with access to certain supplies they can share, such as staplers, hole punchers, scissors, rulers, paper clips, erasers, tape, and so on. Place these items in a central location that is easy for students to reach. Inexpensive hanging bags for shoes (with clear plastic pockets) make excellent supply holders. Simply label and fill each pocket with the appropriate supplies and hang the bag on a low hook or on the back of a door. Or, take a flat cardboard tray (cut from a box) and place the items in the bottom of the tray for students to use. Be sure to trace and label supplies separately so that students remember to return them where they belong.

Paper Goods

Storing paper is easy! Simply purchase or make a small paper tray with multiple compartments for paper storage (available at many teacher supply, stationery, or office supply stores). Place the tray on a counter or table. Divide the paper by colors and store each color separately.

If lack of tabletop or countertop space is an issue, use a file cabinet drawer. Divide the papers into categories by color and place them in separate hanging file folders. If papers are to be used by students, be sure to keep the drawer unlocked and store the papers in a low drawer so that they can easily see which colors they are selecting.

You may also want to have a special box to collect recycled paper or unused reproducibles that students can use for drawing, writing, or brainstorming. Make sure you give clear instructions to the class about which kind of paper is available for them to use, and which kind of paper is for the teacher only.

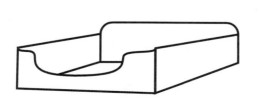

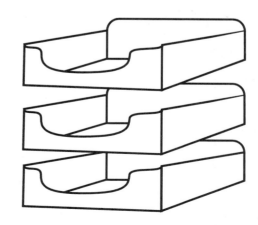

0-7682-2608-2 *Great Rooms! Grades 2–3*

Art Supplies

Second and third graders tend to enjoy art, drawing, and coloring with markers and crayons. Keep a large supply of scissors, glue, paints, crayons, and markers handy for students to use. Arrange the items in an art center, cabinet, or table, and allow students to have access to the supplies. Or, give students each a plastic tub with a lid, labeled on the outside with their name. Have them fill the tub with art supplies from home, such as crayons, markers, glue, scissors, stamps, and so on. Store the tubs on a bookshelf for use in the classroom.

Charts and Posters

Instructional or motivational charts and posters are often bulky and hard to store. Stacking them on top of one another takes less space, but makes the individual posters difficult to find when you need them. Here are tips for solving this problem.

First, laminate the charts and posters before using them so they will not fade or collect dust in your classroom. If you have a storage closet, hang your charts on skirt hangers that have clips at the top. (Three- or four-tiered skirt hangers make excellent poster hangers.) Charts are kept crisp, clean, and easy to find! Or, roll up charts or posters and secure them together at the top with a sturdy clothespin. Label the clothespin so you can easily find specific posters without having to unroll each one. Store them together in a bag or basket in the corner of your room.

0-7682-2608-2 *Great Rooms! Grades 2–3*

Classroom Library

Establishing a library stocked with a wide variety of interesting books is essential for encouraging reading in your classroom. Set up a reading corner with a nice-sized, easy-to-reach bookshelf for storage. Add beanbag chairs, a small couch, or large floor pillows to make the space more inviting and comfortable for students. You may even want to create a theme around your classroom library and give the area a fun name. For example, the Reading Rainforest could be decorated with fake plants and vines hanging from the ceiling. The more creative you are, the more your classroom library will entice children to the area and encourage them to enjoy reading on their own!

Books on Display

Highlighting certain books each week is a great method for encouraging children to expand their reading interest. At the beginning of each week, look through your classroom library and select five or six books to put on display on a shelf or table. Take a few minutes to give a brief introduction of the plot or topic of each book. You may even want to read the publisher's blurb on the back covers of books to spark students' interest. Within a month, turn the task over to the students by allowing a few students each week to select their favorite books to highlight from the classroom library. Then watch those books fly off the shelf as children take a renewed interest in them!

Classroom Library Agreement

It is important that students understand and acknowledge that caring for books in your classroom library is their responsibility. To impress this point upon students and parents, you may want to reproduce a copy of Classroom Library Agreement on page 26 for each child and send it home to be signed by the student and a parent. As the year progresses, periodically remind students of their responsibility and agreement to take good care of the books in your classroom.

Classroom Library Agreement

Checking out books from our classroom library is a privilege. It is important that each student understands and accepts the responsibility of caring for the books before using our classroom library.

By signing this agreement, you are showing that you understand the following:

- It is my responsibility to take good care of the books in our classroom library.
- Books that I check out from our classroom library are to be returned in good condition.
- I must return the books I check out from the classroom library by the end of the day on _____ of every week.
- Books should be placed neatly on the shelf—right side up, with the spine of the book facing outward.
- If a book from our classroom library is damaged or lost while under my care, I must pay to replace the book or work out a plan with my teacher.

Signed,

_____   _____
Student Signature   *Date*

Signed,

_____   _____
Parent Signature   *Date*

0-7682-2608-2 *Great Rooms! Grades 2–3*

Lost and Found

Throughout the course of the year, some students may lose track of their belongings and other students will find items that do not belong to them. Rather than interrupt valuable instructional time to sort out these items, you may want to utilize one of these methods for handling lost and found objects in your classroom.

Lost and Found Tub

Set a large tub or dishpan on a counter or table, or in a corner of the room. Label the tub "Lost and Found" and encourage students to deposit in the tub any items that they find. Allow students who have misplaced or lost their belongings to search through the tub at lunchtime or at the end of the school day.

Lost and Found Board

Set up a bulletin board titled "Lost and Found." Reproduce several copies of page 28, cut apart the notices, and place them in separate folders. Label the folders and staple them to the bottom of the bulletin board. Encourage students who have lost something to fill out and post a *Lost!* notice on the bulletin board for other students to see. Likewise, encourage students who have found an object that does not belong to them to fill out and post a *Found!* notice.

This system will allow students the opportunity to recover their misplaced belongings while practicing descriptive writing! At the end of each week, be sure to review the notices that are on the board and take down notices that are no longer needed.

 # LOST!

Item: _____

Description: _____

_____

_____

It belongs to _____

It was last seen _____

_____

If you see this item, please notify the owner at once!

FOUND!

Item: _____

Description: _____

_____

_____

_____

Who found it _____

If you own this item, please notify the finder at once!

0-7682-2608-2 *Great Rooms! Grades 2–*

Chapter 2: Classroom Management

As many seasoned teachers already know, how you manage your classroom is just as important as the subjects that you teach. Setting the tone for classroom management on the first day of school will determine how smoothly your classroom will run for the rest of the year! Take time to establish rules and clearly communicate consequences so that students understand what behavior is expected of them in your classroom.

This chapter includes ideas for:

- establishing rules
- setting rewards and consequences
- attention moves
- quieting signals
- discipline techniques
- documenting student behavior
- communicating expectations

Establishing Rules

Students need limits in order to function effectively in a school environment. Establishing rules on the first day of school will set the tone for your classroom and help children understand your expectations from the start.

Keep It Simple

For second and third graders, rules should be simple, limited in number, and easy to remember. Keeping the number of rules to a minimum will increase the likelihood of students remembering your classroom rules quickly so that they are accountable for following them. By the end of the second or third day of class, students should be able to recite the classroom rules without looking at the printed list. The advantage to this is that students will automatically know when they have broken a rule and will easily be able to understand why they are receiving consequences. Complicated rules confuse children and may create insecurity and fear.

Post Classroom Rules

It is important to post classroom rules in a prominent location in your classroom. Not only will this serve as a reminder for students, but also it will provide parents and other school visitors with a quick reference of your behavioral expectations for the students in your class. Having a posted list of rules also helps students remember each rule and allows you to hold students accountable when their behavior choices do not match up to the standards you have set.

Positive Over Negative

While it is easy to make a list of behaviors that you would like students *not* to do, this sets a negative tone for your classroom. Instead, try encouraging children to do the right thing by clearly stating the behavior you would like for them to exhibit. For example, instead of stating the rule "No talking in class," give a specific rule explaining when it is okay to talk, such as "Raise your hand for permission to speak." This gives students a clear and realistic picture of your expectations. You may find that you need to clarify a rule by using a negative instruction, such as "No teasing or cursing" in the sample poster on the next page, but try not to make this your focus in establishing your classroom rules.

Classroom Rules

1. Follow directions.

2. Raise your hand for permission to speak.

3. Keep hands, feet, and other objects to yourself.

4. Be respectful of others. (No teasing or cursing.)

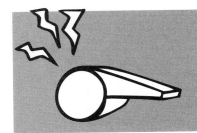

Teaching Classroom Rules

For maximum success in classroom management, rules should be taught on the first day of school and reinforced every day for the first two weeks. The more students are exposed to these rules, the more likely they will be to learn them and begin holding each other accountable for following them.

First, start by stating and explaining each rule. Example: *Our first classroom rule is "Follow directions." This means that if a teacher or another adult in our classroom tells you to do something, you are expected to do it right away.*

Next, give students a concrete example of the rule in practice. Ask a student volunteer to role-play with you. Give the student a directive, such as this: *Please stand, push in your chair, and line up at the door.* Have the class watch as the volunteer follows your directions. If the student follows your directions immediately, praise their efforts: *Thank you. You did a nice job of following directions.* If they deviate from your instructions, correct their actions and direct them to try again: *You did not push in your chair. Please return to your desk and push in your chair, then go back to the door and line up. Thank you.*

Clarifying your rules by offering further explanation and examples helps students to grasp the concept behind each rule and leaves no questions about your expectations. Continue this process to teach the remaining classroom rules. Remind students of these rules at every opportunity so that children understand that you intend to enforce them at all times.

Teaching Classroom Rules
- State
- Explain
- Demonstrate
- Reinforce

0-7682-2608-2 *Great Rooms! Grades 2–*

Setting Rewards and Consequences

Students are very observant. If they see other students break a rule, yet see that there are no consequences for the violators, this quickly teaches them that following classroom rules is "optional." Therefore, when establishing rules for second and third graders, there must be consequences, or penalties, in order for rules to be enforced. It is also helpful to have rewards in order to encourage those who are "caught" following the rules to continue to do so.

Consequences or Penalties

It is important to post your consequences or penalties on the first day of school so that students have a clear, indisputable understanding of what happens to them if they choose to break a rule. Framing the language in terms of "choice" reminds students that they are in control of their behavior and responsible for their own actions.

In explaining consequences to second and third graders, you may want to use outside examples to which they can relate. For example, tell students this: *In soccer, if a player other than the goalie touches the ball with his or her hands, that player is not following the rules. As a result, the player will receive a penalty or consequence for breaking the rule. The same is true in our classroom. If you choose to break a rule, there will be a consequence.*

Explain the consequences to the students. Post the list of consequences near your classroom rules so that students can easily find them. Make sure that your consequences are reasonable and make sense to the students. For example, a first violation should not result in the student being sent to the principal's office. This is not a reasonable consequence to breaking a classroom rule. Instead, consequences should increase incrementally with each violation. Page 34 shows a sample list of consequences that you may want to consider. Reproduce the *Student Behavior Journal* on page 35 if you would like to use it as a consequence.

Follow Through

Once you have established the consequences for breaking classroom rules, you will need to make a conscious effort to consistently follow through. Some students will test the limits of their teacher. In order to maintain positive classroom management throughout the year, it is essential that you give consequences immediately following a violation.

© McGraw-Hill Children's Publishing

0-7682-2608-2 *Great Rooms! Grades 2–3*

Rewards

If you choose to follow the rules . . .

1. Verbal praise

2. Stickers or stamps

3. Extra computer time!

4. Free time!

5. Positive note or phone call to parent

Consequences

If you choose to break a rule . . .

1. Warning

2. Loss of recess time

3. Behavior journal

4. Note or phone call to parent

5. Sent to principal

0-7682-2608-2 *Great Rooms! Grades 2–3*

Student Behavior Journal

Name: _____

Date: _____

The rule I broke was: _____

_____

Next time I will: _____

_____

Student Behavior Journal

Name: _____

Date: _____

The rule I broke was: _____

_____

Next time I will: _____

_____

Effective Methods for Distributing Consequences

Oftentimes, teachers make the mistake of stopping a lesson to give a consequence. While it is important to give a consequence immediately after a rule is broken, it is not necessary to disrupt the class in order to do so. In fact, you may find that disrupting the class to correct a student only reinforces the negative behavior by giving attention to the student. Instead, utilize quiet methods of alerting students that they are not following a rule without taking valuable instruction time away from the class. The following are some effective methods for quietly distributing consequences.

Chalkboard or Whiteboard

Instead of calling out a student's name when you see them exhibiting a behavior that conflicts with your classroom rules, simply write their name on a designated space on the chalkboard or whiteboard. This will alert the student to correct their behavior, while quietly reminding others to keep their behavior in check. At the same time, it will allow you to continue with your lesson with minimum interruption. At the end of the class period, you may want to privately remind the student which rule they were violating and what consequence they will receive. As soon as the student has fulfilled the consequence, remove their name from the board.

Behavior Chart

Using a marker, divide a large piece of poster board into four equal sections. Label each section with the number for each of the rewards for positive student behavior that you have in your classroom. (Example: 1 for verbal praise, 2 for stickers or stamps, and so on.) Then place several Velcro® dots in each section of the poster board and display it in the front of the classroom. Write each child's name on an index card and place a matching dot fastener on the back of each card. If a child follows a rule, remove their card from the stack and attach it to the poster board under the appropriate number. At the end of the class period, praise the students whose names are on the poster board and fulfill their reward. Accentuating positive consequences sets a positive atmosphere that other students will want to model.

Consequence Color Cards

Cut card-sized rectangles from four different colors of paper: blue, yellow, orange, and red. Explain to students that blue represents a warning, yellow represents yield (or first consequence), orange represents caution (or second consequence), and red represents stop (or final consequence). Keep these color cards at the front of the room or at an accessible location on your desk. During a lesson, if any students break a rule, simply place a card on the corner of their desk as a reminder to correct their behavior.

Establishing a Reward System

Just as consequences deter students from breaking rules, rewards will encourage students to follow them. It is not necessary for rewards to be elaborate. But, whether the praise is verbal or tangible, it is helpful for you to recognize and appreciate in some way students' choices to comply with your rules in order to reassure them that they are doing the right thing.

To avoid the tone of bribery, try having students work toward a weekly goal. This gives students something to look forward to, but also allows them to realize that good behavior is more about respect for oneself and others than obtaining prizes and goodies. Post your rewards next to the consequences so that students can read the behavior incentives for themselves. Be consistent and prompt when reinforcing positive behavior. Remember to always follow through on promises made.

Here are some examples of appropriate rewards:

- Verbal praise
- Stickers or stamps
- Extra computer time
- Free time
- Grab bag of small items, such as pencils, rulers, pocket games
- Choice of centers at center time
- Positive note to parent
- Lunch with the teacher
- Positive phone call to parent
- Breakfast with teacher before school
- Behavior chart acknowledging positive behavior

0-7682-2608-2 *Great Rooms! Grades 2–3*

Attention Moves

Occasionally during a lesson, you may find that a student is misbehaving, daydreaming, or simply not paying attention to what is going on in the classroom. It is helpful to practice some attention moves that will engage the student in the lesson without disturbing instruction or distracting the rest of the class.

Close Proximity

If you notice that a student is not on task or not listening during a lesson, continue with your instruction or discussion, but begin walking toward that student's desk. Stop directly in front of or beside the student, but do not stop your lesson. Make eye contact with the student and smile as you continue. Most students will get the message that you have noticed they need additional attention and will immediately become more alert to what is going on in the classroom. With this method, you are just bringing the student back into the lesson without embarrassing them, simply by placing yourself in close proximity to the student.

Using a Student's Name

Another strategy for gaining a student's attention without disrupting your instruction time is to use that student's name in an example or as part of the lesson. For instance, if you see that Nathan is not paying attention in math class, you might say, *If Nathan had fourteen dollars and he spent five dollars, how many dollars would Nathan have left?* In hearing their own names, students often snap to attention and are immediately tuned in to what is being said. Other students, however, will simply regard the use of a student's name as part of the lesson and are unlikely to be at all disturbed or disrupted by the example.

Asking Questions

You can also engage distracted students by asking questions that involve their feedback. However, avoid putting students on the spot by calling on several students to consider a question and then having one of those students volunteer to supply the answer. For example, if you see that Dana is not paying attention, you redirect her attention by saying, *Mike, Dana, or Juan—what type of punctuation mark appears at the end of a command?* Allow these students to consider the question and provide the answer. This will alert Dana that she needs to participate and listen carefully during the rest of the lesson.

Quieting Signals

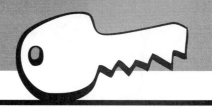

Establishing an understood quieting signal helps to quiet even the noisiest classroom in less than ten seconds. Whether your students are working together on group projects or talking before an assembly, it is essential to have an effective method for quieting students and getting their attention. Shushing students or yelling over their voices is often ineffective, wastes time, and looks as though you have no classroom control. Introducing students to a quieting signal that is used consistently will allow you to quickly quiet the class and gain students' attention whenever you need it. The following are a few ideas you may want to use for your quieting signal.

Regardless of the method you choose to use, be sure to rehearse the procedure many times throughout the first week of school and do not start giving instructions until all students have followed the procedure correctly. If you begin talking before all students are still or quiet, students will get the message that it is not necessary for all of them to comply. Therefore, take the extra time to reinforce that you want all students' attention by waiting for each one to correctly demonstrate your quieting routine.

Lights Out

Explain to students that you will turn the lights off and then on again to signal that you would like them to be quiet and direct their attention to you. Because this is a visual cue, it is not necessary to say anything or shush anyone when you turn the lights off and on. Before allowing students to work in groups or learning centers, explain, *You may talk in your groups, but when I flip the lights off and back on, that is your signal to stop talking, turn to face me, and listen for instructions*. It is important to describe exactly what you want children to do so that they are not moving, talking, or facing the wrong way when you need their attention. Practice the procedure and commend students when they correctly demonstrate the routine.

Commanding Attention

Thumbs Up

Unlike the "Lights Out" method, this procedure can be used inside or outside the classroom. Simply hold your thumbs up in the air and say, *Thumbs up!* When students hear and see this directive, they should drop what they are doing, put their thumbs up in the air, face you, and listen for instructions. This procedure requires students to stop doing tasks such as cutting, pasting, writing, or anything else that keeps their hands busy and distracted. When all thumbs are in the air, ask students to put their hands down to their sides or in their laps and listen carefully.

0-7682-2608-2 *Great Rooms! Grades 2–3*

Commanding Attention

Hand Clap

For an auditory cue, clap your hands twice and have students echo your hand clap. Or devise a clapping rhythm pattern for your class, such as long-long-short-short-short, that students will echo. Continue repeating and echoing with students until all students are participating in the hand clap (about five to eight seconds). After the students echo the clap for the last time, say, *Thank you*, very loudly, and then begin giving your instructions. Be sure to instruct students to sit or stand quietly until you are finished giving instructions.

See and Do

This method relies on students' observation skills. Stand in front of the room and place your hands on your head, saying quietly, *If you can hear me, put your hands on your head*. At first, only a few students may hear and follow this instruction. Continue by changing the position of your hands, placing them on your shoulders and saying, *If you can hear me, put your hands on your shoulders*. As more students stop talking to follow your instructions, others will begin to observe what they are doing and follow suit.

Alternate between your head, shoulders, hips, and knees. End by having students place their hands in their laps to wait for your instructions.

Hand Count

Using a hand count signal is another effective method that involves students in the procedure. As students are working in groups or talking to one another, hold up your hand, one finger at a time, and begin counting, *One, two…* As soon as students notice your signal, have them count along with you,… *three, four, five*. When you reach the number five, all students should have their eyes on you, waiting for your instructions.

Teacher Partners

Colleagues can often be a great source of assistance in dealing with disciplinary issues in the classroom. Arrange to partner with a teacher near your classroom. Make an agreement with the teacher that allows each of you to support the other's discipline plan. If a child in your room is misbehaving or distracting others during seatwork time, have the student take their assignment to your partner's room to work. Be sure to arrange a quiet space in your own classroom at a table or desk away from other children, to house a student of your colleague as well. This change of scenery will often help students correct the problem and complete their assignments.

Visits to the Office

A big mistake that many teachers make is sending children to the principal's office too quickly and too often. Students who are sent to the principal's office every day or for minor infractions will get the message that this is part of a routine, and the visit will fail to have any impact on their behavior.

In addition, your school administrators are there to help, but they cannot afford to spend all of their time immersed in classroom behavior issues. Sending a daily stream of students to the principal's office as a method of discipline is likely to give administrators the impression that you lack classroom management skills and have no control in your classroom. This becomes burdensome to the principal, who may become less enthusiastic in supporting your discipline plan.

Sending students to the office should be a last step on your discipline plan that is used only in extreme cases. This gives students a clear message that, as the teacher, you are capable of enforcing the rules in your classroom. Having several steps along the way, including a step that involves parents, will encourage them to correct their behavior before reaching a last resort of a visit to the principal's office. Generally speaking, the fewer students in your class who visit the principal's office, the more of an impact the pending threat of such action will have on the behavior of students.

Calling Home

Many teachers are nervous about making a phone call to a student's home. This is usually because the phone call brings bad news. However, if you provide parents with your classroom rules and discipline plan ahead of time, it is almost painless to obtain their cooperation and support when it is time for them to play a role in enforcing the rules with their children.

Most parents want their children to behave and follow classroom rules, and they welcome the opportunity that you give them to get involved with their child's education.

When you call parents, be sure to introduce yourself as their child's teacher in a friendly and approachable manner. Practice giving a brief introduction while smiling into the phone so that your voice has a pleasant tone. After all, no matter how frustrated you may be with the situation, the parent to whom you are speaking will be part of the solution if you approach the conversation with goodwill and a caring attitude.

Next, explain to the parent that you enjoy having their child in class, but unfortunately, you are calling to discuss the child's behavior choices in class today. Be sure to review with the parent the steps you and the student have already taken to correct the problem (the first time they were given a warning, the second time they were given a time out at recess, and the third time they were required to write in the behavior journal).

Tactfully inquire if the child is experiencing any difficulties at home that you could help with at school. A child may be acting out at school due to family problems—illness, job loss, addiction, divorce, and so on.

Share with the parent that you have confidence that their child will work to correct the behavior, but you wanted to alert them to the struggles that the student had today so that the parent could provide some encouragement at home. Ask the parent to discuss the behavior with the child and encourage the child to follow through on their responsibility for following the rules in the classroom.

At the close of the phone call, politely thank the parent for their time and support. If desired, arrange a time in the near future for a follow-up call or in-person meeting. Remember to give parents an update. Parents like to hear good news about their children, too!

0-7682-2608-2 *Great Rooms! Grades 2–3*

Documenting Student Behavior

Teacher-Documented Behavior Assessments

There will be plenty of opportunities to correct students' negative behavior choices through the use of the steps in your discipline plan. However, do not forget to take a few minutes each week to give a note of praise or encouragement to those students who are choosing to follow the rules. (See the reproducible awards on page 45.) Sending home a note like this is also pleasing to parents. It lets them know that you are interested in celebrating their child's accomplishments and in encouraging their child to succeed. A small gesture like a positive phone call or e-mail just to share a special moment between you and a child goes a long way in building positive home-school relationships.

Student-Documented Behavior Assessments

One effective method for encouraging students with discipline struggles is to enlist their help in monitoring their own behavior. At the end of each day, have students fill out a daily progress form or a self-evaluation of their attitudes and performance in school. (See reproducible forms on page 46.) Promoting this sense of self-awareness may help students to correct minor problems in attitude, behavior, and work effort before they develop into major ones. Have parents sign the forms and return them to school each day.

Behavior Log

In order to stay organized and have an accurate record of discipline issues, you may want to keep a behavior log for the students in your class. (See reproducible form on page 47.) Each time an action is taken for the child, record the information in the log. This information will come in handy when you meet with parents for parent-teacher conferences and will allow you to stay on top of rewards and consequences for each child.

Here's the Scoop!

You are out of this world!

'Hat's off to you!

The Cat's Meow!

45

Student Behavior Assessment

Name _____ Date _____

My Daily Progress

Today, my ATTITUDE was…

    excellent   good   OK   poor

Today, my BEHAVIOR was…

    excellent   good   OK   poor

Today, my WORK EFFORT was…

    excellent   good   OK   poor

Comments: _____

_____

_____   _____
Teacher's signature   *Parent's Signature*

Name _____ Date _____

My School Day

Today, I read: _____

_____

I worked on: _____

_____

Tomorrow, I will try to: _____

_____

_____   _____
Teacher's signature   *Parent's Signature*

0-7682-2608-2 *Great Rooms! Grades 2–3*

STUDENT BEHAVIOR LOG

Date	Student's Name	Rule Violated/Positive Behavior	Action Taken	Comments

0-7682-2608-2 *Great Rooms!* Grades 2–3

Communicating Expectations

Once you have decided on your rules, consequences, rewards, and discipline plan and explained the plan to your students, you will need to communicate these expectations to the parents and school administrator as well. This is necessary in order to ensure that you are supported in your actions.

If you send a student to the principal's office, it is important for the principal to know that the student has received four prior consequences for inappropriate behavior in the classroom. If you provide your principal with a copy of your rules and consequences, that administrator will automatically understand that a student who is sent to the office has committed multiple infractions of your classroom rules. This will allow the principal to partner with you in confidently administering an appropriate consequence to the student.

Likewise, alerting the parents to your expectations and discipline plan will enable you to enlist their help and support if you need to contact them about their child's behavior infractions. (See the sample parent letter on page 49.) Having a copy of your rules, rewards, and consequences allows parents to be fully informed about the expectations you have for their children. If you contact parents to discuss a behavior problem, they will know that their child has received three prior consequences for inappropriate behavior in your classroom.

Finally, be sure that you not only verbally explain the classroom rules to your students, but give them a written copy of your expectations as well. Keep the tone positive and upbeat, conveying to students your confidence in their ability to make appropriate choices and comply with classroom rules. (See the sample student letter on page 50.)

0-7682-2608-2 *Great Rooms! Grades 2–3*

Sample Parent Letter

Dear Parents,

The following is a list of rules that all children in our class are expected to follow. The rules in our class are kept to a minimum so that they are clear and easy for your child to remember. These rules are designed to encourage each student to respect teachers and staff, fellow students, and themselves.

Students are held responsible for knowing the rules that are posted in the classroom, and it is my expectation that each of the students will choose to follow these rules.

Rules

1. Follow directions.
2. Raise your hand for permission to speak.
3. Keep hands, feet, and other objects to yourself.
4. Be respectful of others. (No teasing or cursing.)

Rewards (if you <u>choose</u> to follow the rules):

1. Verbal praise
2. Stickers or stamps
3. Extra computer time!
4. Free time!
5. Positive note or phone call to parent

Consequences (if you <u>choose</u> to break a rule):

1. Warning
2. Loss of recess time
3. Behavior journal
4. Note or phone call to parent
5. Sent to principal

I strive to be consistent in implementing rewards and consequences in the classroom, as it is my aim to instill both a sense of pride and responsibility in each child. Please feel free to contact me with any questions or concerns you may have regarding the rules of our class. Thank you in advance for your support.

Sincerely,

_____

0-7682-2608-2 *Great Rooms! Grades 2–3*

Sample Student Letter

Dear Students,

Welcome to our class! I am looking forward to an exciting year together. As an important member of our class, you will be expected to know and follow the rules. Following these rules shows respect for other students, teachers, and yourself! I know that each of you will do your best to choose to follow these rules.

Rules
1. Follow directions.
2. Raise your hand for permission to speak.
3. Keep hands, feet, and other objects to yourself.
4. Be respectful of others. (No teasing or cursing.)

Rewards (if you <u>choose</u> to follow the rules):
1. Verbal praise
2. Stickers or stamps
3. Extra computer time!
4. Free time!
5. Positive note or phone call to parent

Consequences (if you <u>choose</u> to break a rule):
1. Warning
2. Loss of recess time
3. Behavior journal
4. Note or phone call to parent
5. Sent to principal

Sincerely,

_____

Chapter 3: Establishing Routines

A routine is an automatic action or practice that you and your students adopt for certain tasks, situations, or circumstances while in the classroom. This chapter will help you teach, rehearse, and reinforce classroom procedures so that they become routines for your students.

Read this chapter to learn about:

- entering the classroom
- morning assignment
- attendance and lunch count
- circle time/morning opening
- classroom helpers
- lining up
- recess, lunch, and afternoon dismissal
- sharpening pencils
- asking for help
- going to the restroom
- "What do we do when we're finished?" dilemmas
- emergency procedures
- substitute teachers

Establishing Classroom Routines

The old adage, "Practice Makes Perfect," applies to many aspects of life, but is especially applicable when working with children to establish classroom routines and procedures. Teaching procedures and establishing routines will require an investment of your time during the first few days—or even weeks—of school, but the results will be well worth your effort. If you take the time to clearly explain, model, and reinforce classroom routines and procedures, students will be far less likely to be confused about how things are to be done in your classroom.

In order to effectively explain the procedures you want students to follow and encourage students to adopt these procedures as a routine, you will need to do these four steps:

- **State** and clearly describe the procedure.

- **Demonstrate** or have a volunteer demonstrate the procedure for students to see.

- **Practice** the procedure as a class.

- **Reinforce** the correct procedure by praising students who follow the procedure correctly and correcting those who do not.

More on Routines

Entering the Classroom

Consider how you would like your students to enter the classroom. Is it okay for them to talk loudly with boisterous energy as they race to their seats excited about the day? Or, do you want your students to enter quietly, orderly, and ready to learn? In order to achieve *your* desired classroom climate, you will need to establish a routine for entering the room.

For example, you might tell your students, *When you enter our classroom, you need to walk into the room, use quiet voices, put away your backpacks and lunchboxes if you have them, and go directly to your seats. This is the procedure I would like you to follow each morning.*

If students are to complete other tasks before going to their seats, such as turning in homework, sharpening pencils, or delivering office papers to your desk, include those instructions in your explanation.

After explaining the procedure, ask a volunteer to demonstrate the routine through role-playing. Next, have all students practice the procedure, and positively reinforce those done correctly.

Morning Assignment

As students enter the classroom, it is a good idea to have a morning activity or assignment that students need to complete at the start of the day. This can be as simple as a daily vocabulary exercise, a logic puzzler, or a word scramble. The point of the morning assignment is to immediately engage students in learning as soon as they enter the classroom. You can post the assignment on the board or have it on students' desks. The expectation is that students will learn that they are responsible for starting the day by working on the assignment before anyone tells them to do so.

Attendance and Lunch Count

Take attendance quickly and quietly while children are engaged in another activity. Calling out students' names in a roll call fashion is not necessary and wastes a great amount of time. As students are completing their morning assignments, quickly look around the room to see who is missing and mark the form accordingly.

If lunch count is required, provide a chart for students to check off. Have students place lunch money envelopes in a labeled box before beginning their morning assignment. Store extra envelopes near the box for children who need them. Once taught, this will become part of the students' routine and you will rarely need to remind them of this procedure.

Circle Time/Morning Opening

When all students arrive and you have taken roll, you may want to gather on a carpeted area of the floor to start the morning as a classroom community. Begin by sharing a story or asking students to respond to a question, such as one of these: *What is your favorite mammal? If you had 100 dollars, how would you spend it?* Use the time to introduce one of the themes or concepts you are going to study throughout the day.

Classroom Helpers

Second and third grade students enjoy taking part in the administrative tasks in the classroom. Think about the tasks that you would like students to help you perform in the classroom, then assign these duties to different students each week. Asking students to take responsibility for these classroom jobs will give them a sense of pride and ownership in your classroom.

Helper Charts

Create a helper chart or bulletin board for your classroom. Have fun with your helper chart themes. (See examples on page 56.) Label the jobs that you would like students to perform in your classroom. Each week, attach a different student's name to the various positions, making sure that every student has a turn at each job.

Here are some suggestions for classroom duties:

Messenger———This student takes messages for you to the office or to other teachers.

Librarian———This student is responsible for organizing the classroom library.

Custodians ———These two students are responsible for picking up trash in the room at the end of each day.

Secretary ———This student posts the new date on the calendar and collects missed work for absent students.

Line Leader ———This student leads the line when students move throughout the school.

Paper Manager—This student helps collect and pass out papers for the teacher.

Class Comedian–This student starts each day by telling a joke to the class.

Substitute ———This student completes the duties of any absent workers.

0-7682-2608-2 *Great Rooms! Grades 2–3*

Helper Bulletin Charts

Mrs. Tate's Team of Helpers

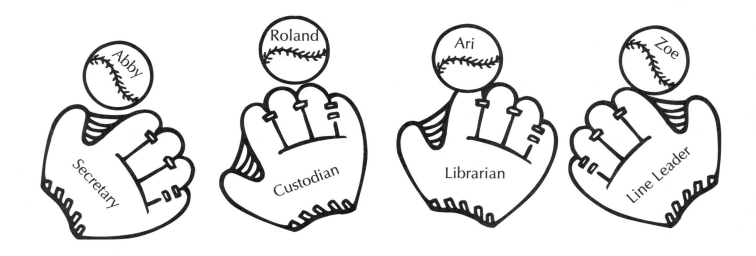

Abby — Secretary
Roland — Custodian
Ari — Librarian
Zoe — Line Leader

Help Wanted!

Help Wanted!

Loreena
Paper Manager

Brant
Secretary

Ramal
Line Leader

Eric
Librarian

Jillian
Custodian

0-7682-2608-2 Great Rooms! Grades 2–3

Baseball and Glove

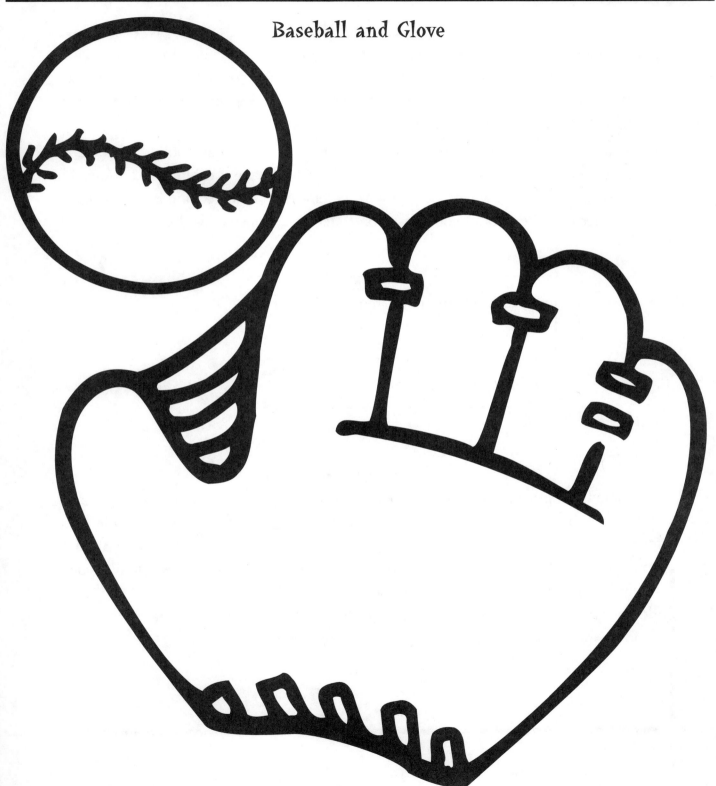

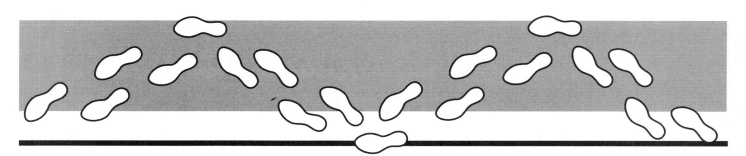

Lining Up

In early elementary grades, teachers often must transport their students from one place to another several times throughout the day. Whether going to lunch, P.E. class, recess, or the school library, it is important that students move in a quiet and orderly manner through the building so as not to disturb other classes.

When leaving the classroom, have a procedure for lining up at the door. It may be a hand signal or verbal directions, or dismissing by rows. Make sure students know how you expect them to behave in line. Remind students of this expectation by displaying a mini-poster near the door of your classroom, such as the one shown here.

When walking in line, remember to…
- Face forward.
- Put hands at your sides.
- Keep mouths quiet.

Follow the Footsteps

Eliminate line-up hassles by creating footstep patterns to show children where to stand. Reproduce the footstep patterns (page 59) on colored paper and cut them out—one set for each child. Label one set of footsteps "Line Leader," and position it three steps back from the door. Place the other sets of footsteps on the floor where you would like your students to line up, leaving an ample amount of space between them. Secure them to the floor using clear heavy tape. As students line up to leave the room, have them stand on the footsteps so that they are in the correct spots!

Footstep Patterns

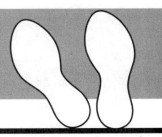

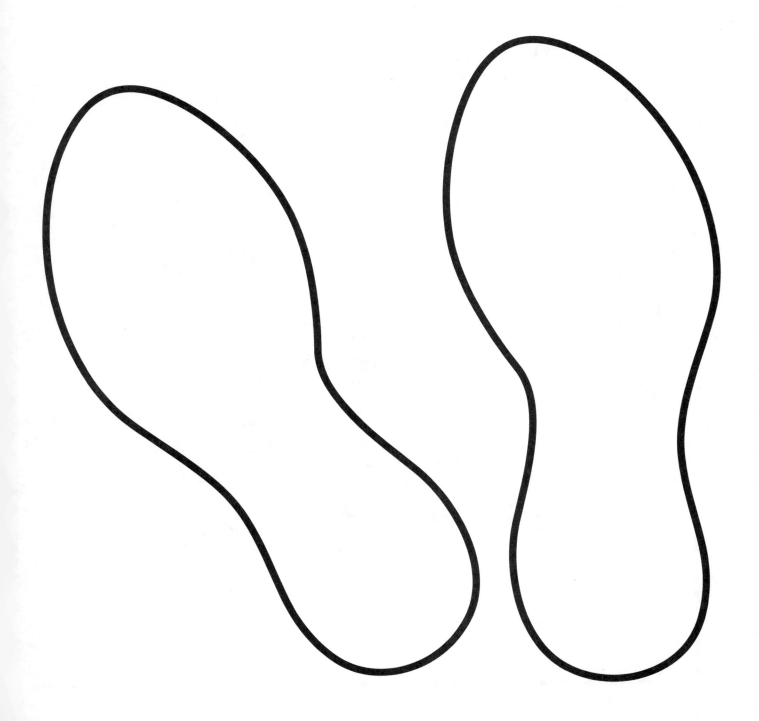

0-7682-2608-2 *Great Rooms! Grades 2–3*

Managing Traffic

Recess, Lunch, and Afternoon Dismissal

Your school may have bells or clocks that signify when it is time to go to recess, lunch, or home for the day. However, if you do not want the children running out the door as you give last minute instructions, make sure they understand that as their teacher *you* are the one who is responsible for dismissing the class. This will enable you to use all of your instructional time to the fullest, without students packing up early and leaving the room before you have completed your lesson or activity.

Sharpening Pencils

If possible, set up an electric pencil sharpener for your students to use. Have students get into the habit of sharpening two pencils every morning before school begins. This will reduce the amount of time that students spend at the sharpener. If constant disruptions are still an issue, encourage students to keep silent, hand-held sharpeners in their desks.

Asking for Help

Second and third grade students will be able to do a significant amount of individual work on their own. However, there will be times when students will need your help completing a task, reading a sentence, or answering a question while doing seatwork. Some teachers prefer to have students form a line at their desk to have questions answered. However, this wastes valuable work time for those who are waiting at the back of the line. It also leaves more opportunities for students to act up out of boredom by poking each other or talking in line. Others prefer to have students raise their hands at their desks to signal that they need help. This method may also be ineffective because students tend to stop working while they dangle their hands in the air, waiting for assistance. This is also a visual distraction for other students. Instead, use a system that allows students to signal that they need help without disrupting others. Here are a few examples:

Tri-Fold Cards

Provide each student with a sheet of construction paper. Show them how to fold the paper in thirds and then unfold it. In the bottom third, have students print this sentence: *I need help*. Next, tell students to turn the paper upside down and in the middle section write this sentence: *Please continue to work*. Then, have students refold the paper and tape the ends together to make a triangle shape that will rest on their desk. As students need help, have them turn the "I need help" side toward you. The other message faces them to remind students to keep working on their assignment while they wait for your assistance.

0-7682-2608-2 *Great Rooms! Grades 2–3*

More on Help

Clothespin Signs

Tape a clothespin securely to the edge of each student's desk. Give each child a red square of construction paper. Anytime a student needs your assistance, have that child clip the red square into the mouth of the clothespin. The red color will be a signal to you to approach the student's desk. Remind students to continue working on other parts of the assignment until you can answer their questions. Once you help the student, remove the red card from the clothespin.

Help Me Hat

It may seem silly, but having students wear a hat to signal that they need your help is a great way for them to get your attention without having to occupy their hands and take time away from their own work. At the beginning of the year, simply give students a strip of construction paper and measure the strip to fit their heads. Staple the ends of the strip together and allow students to decorate the hats. As students need help, have them put on the hat and continue to work until you come to their desk.

Going to the Restroom

It is a fact of life that students will need to go to the restroom at one time or another while they are in your classroom. Rather than continually having students disrupt your lesson or interrupt other students to ask permission to leave the classroom, make the process as easy and unobtrusive as possible.

Reproduce and cut apart the two restroom passes on page 64. Glue each one separately onto heavy cardstock, then laminate them. Punch a hole in the top of each one and tie a length of string through it so students can wear the pass around their neck. Hang each restroom pass on a separate nail or hook in a visible position next to the door of the classroom.

Explain to students that if they need to go to the restroom, they should first look to see that a pass is available. If the pass is there, they may quietly get up, take the pass, and exit the classroom door. This way, students may take restroom breaks without disturbing the rest of the class and you will always know if a student has left the room since a pass will be gone.

If you would like, you can stipulate when the pass can be used. For example, you may want to instruct children that they are only to go to the restroom during seat work or center time, but not while you are giving instructions. You may also attempt to limit restroom breaks to lunch and recess time, but this may not be a realistic expectation for young children. Make sure that students know that they should return to the classroom promptly.

0-7682-2608-2 *Great Rooms! Grades 2–3*

Restroom Passes

Girls' Restroom Pass

Teacher: _____

Grade: _____

Boys' Restroom Pass

Teacher: _____

Grade: _____

0-7682-2608-2 *Great Rooms! Grades 2–3*

"What Do We Do When We're Finished?" Dilemmas

In planning your lessons, you will need to allow ample time for teacher-instruction, modeling, guided practice, and independent practice in order for students to master new material. The amount of time needed for independent practice will vary among the students in your class. In order to allow most students to have enough time to complete independent assignments without being interrupted by their peers who are finished, it is important to have a procedure for students to follow when they have completed an assignment.

Enrichment Centers

You may want to set up a quiet learning center complete with enrichment activities for students to complete when they are finished with a given assignment. This center should be filled with a variety of student-directed, easy-to-follow activities, such as crossword puzzles, vocabulary exercises, reading comprehension cards, or math logic problems. Direct students to select an activity from the center and take it their desks to work quietly while other students are completing work.

Independent Reading

Encourage all students to be prepared for "waiting time" in your classroom. Rather than providing students with additional activities to complete after they are finished with independent work, have them read a book! Ask all students to keep a chapter book at their desk to read during these waiting times.

Creative Solutions

Challenge your students to come up with their own ideas for activities to keep them busy after they have finished an assignment. Brainstorm a list with the class and post it in a prominent location in the classroom. Or, provide them with a copy of page 66 and invite them to choose one of these solutions when they are finished with work.

Things to Do When You're Done

1. **Work on art project—draw or watercolors**

2. **Read a book or magazine**

3. **Study for upcoming test**

4. **Do a free-write journal entry**

5. **Card game**

6. **Make flash cards of spelling words**

7. **Practice math facts**

8. **Finish homework or another project**

9. **Tangram problem**

10. **Crossword or jigsaw puzzle**

0-7682-2608-2 *Great Rooms! Grades 2–3*

Emergency Procedures

Establish emergency procedures for your classroom during the first week of school. Make sure that children have a clear understanding of what circumstances constitute an emergency (fire, earthquake or other natural disaster, security situation). If the procedure is different for each circumstance, walk students through the process until all students are comfortable that they know what to do in case of an emergency.

What Do We Do?

Explain to students that in emergency situations people sometimes forget to remain calm. Tell them that we practice what to do in case of an emergency so that the action is automatic and overrides our tendency to panic. Be sure students know that they are to remain calm and leave the building quickly and quietly with no running or pushing. Remind them that your first job is to make sure that they always feel safe.

Where Do We Go?

Set up a meeting place for your class to go in case of an emergency. Your school probably has a school-wide plan that designates this spot for you on campus. Find out where it is, take your class to visit the location, and make sure that you review the location with them several times. Tell students that in case of emergency you will walk them together to that location. If they should somehow get separated from the group, they are to meet you at the emergency location. Point out that students may need to go to a different outside location if they are in another part of the building (cafeteria, library, art room, etc.) when the drill or emergency occurs. Reassure students that the staff member in charge wherever they may be will direct them on where to go.

Who Is in Charge?

Students should understand that, as their teacher, you will be in charge of the classroom in case of an emergency. Explain that they will need to look to you for special instructions and follow your directions to safety. However, it is a good idea to appoint one or two students who will be responsible for getting help if you are incapacitated during an emergency. Instruct those children to find the nearest teacher or administrator for assistance.

Contact Forms

At the beginning of the year, have parents fill out the *Classroom Emergency Contact Form* on page 68. Place these forms in alphabetical order in a backpack along with a small first aid kit and carry the backpack with you anytime you leave the classroom. This allows you to be prepared in an emergency.

© McGraw-Hill Children's Publishing 0-7682-2608-2 *Great Rooms! Grades 2–3*

Emergency Contact Form

Child's Name: _____

Date of Birth: _____

Allergies or Medical Conditions: _____

_____

Mother's Contact Information

Name of Mother/Guardian: _____

Home Address: _____

Daytime Phone: _____ Evening Phone: _____

Cell Phone: _____

Father's Contact Information

Name of Father/Guardian: _____

Home Address: _____

Daytime Phone: _____ Evening Phone: _____

Cell Phone: _____

Other Emergency Contact: _____

Relation to student: _____

Daytime Phone: _____ Evening Phone: _____

Cell Phone: _____

Physician's Name: _____

Physician's Phone: _____

0-7682-2608-2 *Great Rooms! Grades 2–3*

Substitute Teacher

From time to time, you may be absent from school due to illness, personal reasons, or professional training. At this time, a substitute teacher will be called in to take your place in the classroom.

Contacting a Substitute Teacher

Your school or district may use a substitute finder service that contacts substitute teachers and arranges daily replacements for you. Or, you may be responsible for finding a substitute on your own by calling names on an approved list. At the beginning of the year, be sure to inquire with the school secretary or a fellow teacher about your school or district policy so you can prepare accordingly and obtain any special codes or instructions for phone messages you may need to input or record.

Preparing Your Class for a Substitute Teacher

At the beginning of the school year, take a few minutes to talk to your class about your expectations regarding their behavior with regard to a substitute teacher. While you may not have advanced notice of your absence, it is important to prepare students for such an event so that they feel comfortable and prepared in the situation.

Explain to students that you do not plan to be absent—but if you are, you have a clear plan that will allow students to continue with their regular school routine until you return. This will help to lessen the anxiety that younger students often feel when they are greeted by a substitute upon their arrival at school.

Substitute Folder

In order to have a successful experience in your classroom, a substitute teacher will need an adequate amount of information about your school, classroom, students, daily schedule, lesson plans, and procedures. To minimize the amount of work you will need to do in case of an unexpected absence, take time at the beginning of the school year to fill out the *Substitute Teacher Information* form on pages 71 and 72. Place the form in a folder marked "For the Substitute" along with copies of page 73, *Class Evaluation Form*. Be sure to place the folder in a handy spot that is easy for administrators or other teachers to find quickly in your absence.

Substitute Cassette Tape

Instead of leaving written instructions, you may want to simply tape-record a message for your substitute teacher. You will still need to leave lesson plans, a seating chart, and other visual information; but a tape-recording allows you to elaborate on plans or give tips on classroom routines and procedures without having to write down every detail.

Substitute's Class Evaluation Form

Leave a Class Evaluation Form for the substitute teacher to fill out at the end of the day. (See page 73.) This conveys that you value the substitute teacher's opinions and want to be informed about the behavior and academic progress of the students in your class during your absence.

Substitute Teacher Information

Thank you for serving as a guest teacher in our classroom. This form contains information that should help you throughout the day.

Today, you are substituting for _____ Grade _____

You can find these items in the following locations:

Lesson plans _____

Teacher manuals _____

Student emergency cards _____

Nearest restroom _____

Teacher's lounge _____

Phone extensions _____

If you need assistance, please contact _____ in room _____.

These are our usual routines/procedures:

Attendance and lunch count _____

_____

Restroom use _____

Recess _____

Lunch _____

Dismissal _____

Emergency or Drills _____

_____

These students leave the classroom to work with a specialist:

_____

_____

_____

Special Schedule Notes

Monday _____

_____

Tuesday _____

_____

Wednesday _____

_____

Thursday _____

_____

Friday _____

The following students are reliable helpers:

_____

_____

_____

Seating Chart:

(Attach a current copy of your classroom seating chart with names of students, if you switch classes, or teach a special class, include these seating charts as well.)

Class Evaluation Form

Dear Substitute,

Welcome to our classroom! I hope you have a great day. Please fill out this form at the end of the day to keep me informed about events that happened in my absence. Thank you!

Sincerely,

_____

Overall, the class behavior was...

Excellent   Good   Fair   Poor

The following students were exceptionally helpful throughout the day: _____

_____

Were there any behavior problems during the day?   Yes   No

If Yes, please explain:

Were there any problems with lessons today?   Yes   No

If Yes, please explain: _____

_____

_____

Additional comments: _____

_____

_____

_____

Substitute's name

Chapter 4: Paperwork

Perhaps one of the most daunting tasks of teaching is keeping up with paperwork. A few stacks of papers can easily turn into an overwhelming pile if not organized and managed well. Clearly, there are as many ways to deal with paperwork as there are teachers, but this chapter will take a look at several effective methods that have been used successfully in the classroom.

This chapter includes ideas for:

- assigning homework
- collecting and returning student work
- managing make-up work
- preparing student portfolios
- assessment
- communicating with parents
- organizing progress reports and report cards

0-7682-2608-2 *Great Rooms! Grades 2–3*

Assigning Homework

Assigning homework for students to complete is an excellent way to measure independent progress and to allow parents to gain a better understanding of the concepts you are covering in your classroom. You will want to make sure your homework is reasonable, in regards to time involved and difficulty. Encourage students to share their homework assignments with parents and to call on them as resources for additional help and explanation.

Homework Assignment Sheets

Reproduce a copy of the *Homework Assignment Sheet* on page 76 for each student. Attach the page to a plain document envelope for each student to carry back and forth from school to home. Have students record homework assignments and due dates on the sheet and place homework reproducibles inside the envelope. Or, give each student a homework folder in which to store assignment sheets and homework pages. Ask parents to initial the sheet every day so they can help their children be accountable for completing the work.

Long-Term Assignments

Long-term assignments can be difficult for second and third grade students. Long-term projects, such as animal reports, often require a large amount of advanced planning and a mastery of time management skills. If you wish to assign a long-term project for your students, you may want to enlist the help and support of their parents. Send a note home explaining the purpose of the project and a suggested time line for completing the various stages. Have frequent checkpoints for your students to meet so that you are aware of their progress and can pinpoint students who may need additional help in completing the project on time.

Read, Read, Read!

Many teachers like to assign independent reading as homework, approximately 20 to 30 minutes a night. In addition to the obvious educational value, this type of homework assignment has the added benefit of being fair to students of all abilities, in regards to the amount of time it takes to complete. If assigning reading as homework matches your teaching style, you may want to periodically include book reviews in the assignment. A twist on the traditional book report, book reviews allow students to act as book critics. Make copies of page 77 and encourage students to complete a book review to share with the class. (These can be used for books in progress, not just finished books.) Take a few minutes every couple of weeks to allow students to give an oral presentation of a book of their choosing. Post the book reviews on a bulletin board as advertisements for other students to see.

Name _____

Homework Assignment Sheet

Date Assigned	Subject/Assignment	Due Date	Parent Initials

0-7682-2608-2 *Great Rooms! Grades 2–3*

Name _____ Date _____

Book Review

Think about a book you are reading or have finished. Answer the questions.

Title of book _____

Author _____

What do you like best about this book? _____

_____

_____

What do you like least? _____

_____

_____

Does/Did the story hold your interest? Why or why not? _____

_____

_____

_____

Would you recommend this book to others? Why or why not? _____

_____

_____

In the space below, draw a picture of a character or a scene that you liked.

McGraw-Hill Children's Publishing

0-7682-2608-2 *Great Rooms! Grades 2–3*

Collecting and Returning Student Work

To help manage your paper flow, establish classroom procedures or routines with regard to collecting class work and homework. Explain the procedures to students and give them opportunities to rehearse the process during the first week of school. Consider the following ideas to streamline the process of collecting paperwork from your students.

Paper Pass

As students complete a class or group assignment, you may want them to pass their papers from their desks to you. However, try to avoid having students pass papers forward from one hand to the next. This procedure, which requires students to pass papers to someone who is not facing them, invites multiple problems among students. Instead, have them pass papers sideways from left to right from one desk to the next.

Paper Monitors

To avoid paper-passing dilemmas altogether, assign two students the job of paper monitor, rotating it on a weekly basis. When students complete classroom assignments, ask the paper monitors to quickly circulate around the room to collect the papers.

Collecting by Number

Make an alphabetical list of the students in your class and assign each student a number that they will use throughout the year. When collecting assignments, call out the numbers in order and have students bring their papers forward in numerical order. This method is a bit more time consuming at first—but with practice, the process is quick and easy. In addition, it keeps papers organized and easy to record and file after grading.

Subject Trays

Acquire and label stackable plastic trays, one for each subject. As students finish an assignment, they can place it in the corresponding tray.

More On Homework

Homework Baskets

Set out a homework basket or tray in a prominent location in your classroom. Label the basket *"HOMEWORK"* and explain to students that they should turn their homework in to this basket every morning. The sooner you establish this procedure, the faster it will become a part of the students' morning routine.

Homework Folders

Another method for keeping track of student homework is to provide each student with a homework folder. Each morning, have students place the folders on your desk or turn them in to a specified location. Or, have students place the folders on the corner of their desks, and collect them one at a time as students complete morning work. This will allow you to see at-a-glance which students have completed their homework and which have not.

Friday Folders

Rather than returning students' papers throughout the week, you may want to hold on to them and return them as a set each Friday. These papers can then be sent home to families in a special "Friday Folder," along with school announcements, forms that need to be signed, or newsletters. Parents will look forward to these folders as a way of keeping abreast of their child's learning. Train students to return the folders each Monday, empty except for forms or correspondence from parents.

Managing Make-Up Work

From time to time, students will be absent from school. In order to help absent students make a smooth transition back into the classroom, try to have missed assignments organized and ready to give to them upon their return.

Give Make-Up Expectations in Writing

To make the process simple, use a standard form (such as the one provided on page 81) for recording assignments that students miss. You may want to allow a student volunteer or class secretary to write and collect the assignments for the missing student. At the end of the day, all make-up work will be assembled with a written record of the assignments that are to be completed. Having a written record helps communicate your expectations to both students and parents.

Set a Deadline

Students are often confused about how much time they have to complete assignments upon their return to school. Set a reasonable time limit and put it in writing so that your expectations are clear. Keep in mind that the student will probably need a few days for each day missed to complete the make-up work and to be able to stay caught up with regular school assignments. Be flexible in the assignments that need to be made up and those that could be skipped so that a child who may not be fully healthy does not become overwhelmed with make-up assignments.

Give Make-Up Work in Advance

In some cases, such as a planned vacation or a family matter, you may have advanced notice of a child's absence. In this circumstance, it is helpful for you and the child to organize make-up assignments or work one-on-one for an upcoming lesson prior to the absence. You may also want to give alternative work, such as sending the class a postcard from the vacation site. Of course, these procedures may take a little advanced planning and extra work on your part, but it is worth the effort if the child can easily assimilate back into the classroom with completed assignments ready to turn in.

While You Were Out...
We Missed You!

Name _____ Today's Date _____

Please complete the following assignments by _____ and turn them into your teacher.

Subject   **Assignment**

Reading _____

Math _____

Writing/Spelling _____

Social Studies _____

Science _____

_____

_____

0-7682-2608-2 *Great Rooms! Grades 2–3*

Preparing Student Portfolios

Student portfolios are a collection of student-produced work that is compiled throughout the year. A showcase of students' progress and achievements, portfolios provide insight into each child's individual learning in your classroom.

Storing Portfolios

When compiling student portfolios, there are a variety of storage options from which to choose. Here are a few ideas to consider:

- **Manila folders**—This is a quick and easy method to use when the majority of work collected is standard-sized paper. Just place the folders in a filing cabinet and slip the papers into the folder when adding to the portfolio.

- **Pocket folders**—A slight variation on the manila folder idea, this storage option allows you to collect a few items in pockets, such as small arts and crafts, student-created games, and so on in addition to paperwork.

- **Boxes**—Cereal boxes or shirt boxes are an interesting alternative to using regular folders. With this option, students can include science projects, hands-on math manipulatives, or other items they want to save in their portfolios in addition to paperwork.

- **Large envelopes**—Perhaps you do not have room in your classroom to store portfolio boxes, but folders are just too small for the work students want to include. Large envelopes are a good solution to this dilemma, as they provide space for a few "extra" items while still being able to fit inside a file cabinet.

Selecting Work

There are many different methods used for determining which samples of student work to place in the portfolios. Some teachers choose to select the samples for the students that show a variety of their skills and talents. Other teachers choose to save certain assignments across the board for each student. While still others allow students to select the work samples that they would like to include.

Generally, whatever method you choose, you will want to make sure that each student's portfolio contains more than one sample from a variety of different subject areas throughout the year. For example, if you choose to include writing samples, select one from the beginning of the year from a math journal, one from the middle of the year from a science experiment log, and one from the later part of the year from a history report. This is the best way to show concrete evidence of a student's progress throughout the year.

Other Materials

In addition to student work, you will want to include other documents in the portfolios, such as lists of books the students have read, students' thoughts about school, and student self-assessments. These provide additional insight regarding students' progress and their interests and attitudes about learning. Reproducible examples of these types of materials are given on pages 84–87.

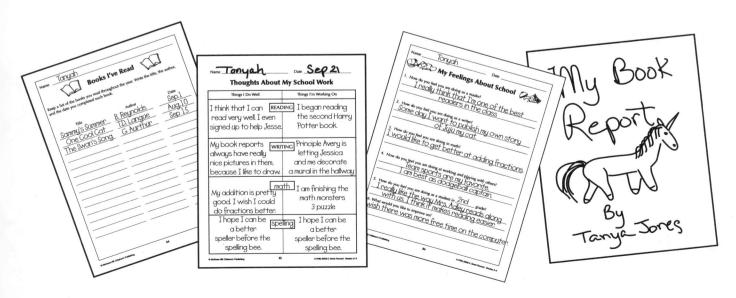

© McGraw-Hill Children's Publishing

83

0-7682-2608-2 *Great Rooms! Grades 2–3*

Name _____

 # Books I've Read

Keep a list of the books you read throughout the year. Write the title, the author, and the date you completed each book.

Title	Author	Date
_____	_____	_____
_____	_____	_____
_____	_____	_____
_____	_____	_____
_____	_____	_____
_____	_____	_____
_____	_____	_____
_____	_____	_____
_____	_____	_____
_____	_____	_____
_____	_____	_____
_____	_____	_____
_____	_____	_____

0-7682-2608-2 *Great Rooms! Grades 2–3*

Name _____ Date _____

Thoughts About My School Work

Things I Do Well	Things I'm Working On
READING	
WRITING	
☐	
☐	

0-7682-2608-2 *Great Rooms! Grades 2–3*

Name _____ Date _____

My Feelings About School

1. How do you feel you are doing as a reader?

_____

_____

2. How do you feel you are doing as a writer?

_____

_____

3. How do you feel you are doing in math?

_____

_____

4. How do you feel you are doing at working and playing with others?

_____

_____

5. How do you feel you are doing as a student in _____ grade?

_____

_____

6. What would you like to improve on?

_____

_____

Student Profile

My full name is _____

My birthday is _____

My favorite color is _____

My favorite food is _____

The sport I like best is _____

My favorite book is _____

The subject I like most in school is _____

I'll bet you didn't know that I like to _____

_____

By the end of the year, I hope I will be able to _____

_____

Here is a picture of me doing something I like:

0-7682-2608-2 *Great Rooms! Grades 2–3*

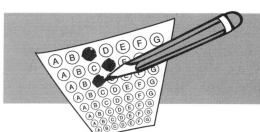

Assessment

As a teacher, one of the most important tasks you will have is to assess student learning. This is sometimes challenging because students often learn and express their understanding in different ways. In order to accommodate these differences and get a true picture of a student's level of mastery, it is essential to use a variety of assessment methods.

Tests

A longstanding staple in our system of education, tests seem to be a quick and easy method for measuring student mastery and performance in a certain subject area. Ideally, before you begin teaching a unit or a lesson, you should have a firm idea of the concepts you would like students to master so that you are clearly teaching what you plan to test. This clarity will help you in structuring your assessment as well as in assisting students in mastering smaller parts of the material along the way. While tests are often effective in getting students to memorize or recite facts and to demonstrate problem-solving skills, they are not always the best method for assessing a student's deeper level of understanding of the concepts.

Portfolios

As discussed in the previous section of this chapter, student portfolios provide more in-depth insight, not only into the student's learning, but also in the progress the student has made throughout the year. Unlike a single test which measures absolutes, a student portfolio allows you to compare the student's demonstrated abilities over time, showing the individual's learning progression from the beginning of the year to the end. For students who perform at the bottom of the class in relation to their peers, this method of assessment is encouraging, as it focuses on forward progress and individual achievement.

Alternative Assessment

Class Discussions

Informal assessments can easily be conducted through your observations during class discussions. Asking questions about a content area and inviting students to respond allows you to obtain immediate feedback and information about the thinking and learning process of many of your students. Be aware, however, that this method does not provide consistent and accurate assessment for all students, as some will be hesitant to participate in class or will forget what they wanted to say once they raise their hands and realize that all eyes are on them. You may want to keep a notebook to document participation, with each student's name on a separate page. Throughout each grading period, jot down notes describing students' participation, insightful comments, or progress in contributing to class discussions.

Games

Some students' nervousness and anxiety causes them to perform poorly on tests or quizzes. Other students are shy and tend to withdraw from classroom participation when the spotlight is on them. However, ask any elementary-age students if they enjoy playing games, and you are sure to receive the answer in a resounding shout of "YES!" For this reason, learning games are a very effective method of assessment. Either played as a class or in small groups, observing student performance as they play games gives teachers a quick insight into the understanding and learning mastery of each player. Best of all, students aren't nervous because they do not even realize their performance is being assessed.

Student-Teacher Conferences

When in doubt, sit down and talk to your students about their learning. Schedule individual student-teacher conferences every couple of weeks. Invite students to sit down with you and talk about their progress in school. How do they feel? What area is giving them trouble? What subject matter do they feel most comfortable with? How can you help them improve? Talking openly with students about their learning will convey to them that you care about their progress and want them to succeed.

0-7682-2608-2 *Great Rooms! Grades 2–3*

Communicating with Parents

Communicating with parents is key to gaining and maintaining a partner-relationship with them throughout the year. When parents are informed, they are much more likely to support the plans, curriculum, and activities that are implemented in your classroom.

To maximize this support and your success in the classroom, take the opportunity to communicate with them through a variety of newsletters.

Be sure to consider the needs of your students whose parents are divorced. Send separate sets of all correspondence to both parents, if possible, to aid them in supporting their child.

Weekly Newsletter

Communicating through a weekly newsletter will allow you to give parents a general overview of the happenings in your class each week. A few short paragraphs describing what you are studying or highlighting special school activities will keep parents informed; and it will enable them to ask their children pointed questions about their school experience throughout the week. In addition, you may want to include a list of homework assignments for each day of the week to serve as a reminder.

If you have a computer, you can set up a simple template in your word processing program. Each week open an existing newsletter file, select "Save As" and rename the file with the current date, and simply type over the text with updated information.

Thematic Newsletter

If you choose to teach your curriculum using thematic units, get parents involved by making them aware of your plans. At the beginning of each thematic study, send home a note asking for materials, ideas, or assistance in supporting your theme. Make suggestions for extending student learning at home and invite parents to participate.

Information Newsletters

Send home an information newsletter periodically throughout the year. In this newsletter, simply select a topic you would like to address (homework, writing, at-home learning activities) and write a friendly letter that provides some tips for parents. (See pages 91 and 92 for sample letters.) Parents will appreciate your effort to give them strategies to help their children succeed in school.

Dear Parents or Guardians,

Part of our goal this year is to learn about responsibility. It is your child's responsibility to complete and turn in homework on time. Here are some handy tips to help your child develop a sense of responsibility with regard to homework.

- Talk with your child about each day's homework assignment. Guide your child in setting aside a specific time and place for completing homework after school.

- Encourage your child to do the homework independently. If your child needs assistance, try asking questions and looking at examples together, rather than just giving the answer. Help your child develop problem-solving skills in order to complete the homework.

- Help your child with organization. Encourage your child to select a designated spot in your home where completed homework can be stored. Keeping assignments in the same place every day will reduce incidences of lost or forgotten work.

- Encourage your child to show you finished homework assignments before going to bed each night.

Homework for my class is designed to take about _____ minutes each day. If you feel your child has too little or too much homework, please contact me.

Thank you for your efforts in developing your child's sense of responsibility.

Sincerely,

_____

Your Child's Teacher

0-7682-2608-2 *Great Rooms! Grades 2–3*

Dear Parents or Guardians,

Our class is working on developing our writing skills. You can help at home by encouraging your child to engage in some of the following writing activities:

- Write a letter to a relative or friend.
- Copy a favorite recipe from a cookbook or create a new recipe.
- Make a list of groceries that you need from the market.
- Write down a schedule of extracurricular activities.
- Interview a parent or another adult about his or her job. Write five questions and have the adult write the answers. Switch roles.
- Make a list of favorites—colors, foods, movies, and so on.
- Create a telephone directory with names, numbers and e-mail addresses of your friends.
- Make a list of fun things to do with your family that are free.
- _____
  _____

Be creative! Encourage your child to add another item to the list!

Thank you for supporting your child's writing development.

Sincerely,

_____

Your Child's Teacher

0-7682-2608-2 *Great Rooms! Grades 2–3*

Sharing Successes

Too often, teachers communicate with parents only when they have something negative to report. This can create the undesirable affect of an adversarial relationship, immediately placing the parent on the defensive. Instead, it is important to communicate students' successes in addition to the areas that need improvement. In the first few weeks of school, make a point to identify and note areas of academic strengths for each child. Send a quick note home (see page 94) during this time to praise the child's effort or achievements.

Handling Difficulties

At the first sign of academic trouble, notify parents and set up a meeting to discuss your concerns. Avoid the temptation to wait until the end of the quarter or grading period to flag these issues or indicate that there is a problem. By then, it is often too late to correct the problem because the student has fallen so far behind. Give parents as much notice as possible and try to provide viable solutions or strategies for correcting and resolving the problem. Parents will appreciate your efforts to help their child succeed.

Parent Feedback

Halfway through the year, reproduce a copy of the *Parent Feedback Form* on page 95 and ask parents to provide you with feedback. After all, you have been charged with educating their children, and they will appreciate the opportunity you provide them to share their child's successes or make suggestions for improvements. This is also a great way for you to check to see that, as a professional educator, you are meeting the individual needs of the students and families in your classroom. Since many schools have conferences at the beginning and end of the year, this midyear checkup helps you achieve the goal of consistent home-school communication.

0-7682-2608-2 *Great Rooms! Grades 2–3*

Something to Cheer About!

Dear _____,

I noticed that _____ did really well

in _____ today. Your child showed an amazing

ability to _____

_____

Please congratulate your child on this positive effort!

Sincerely,

_____

Something to Cheer About!

Dear _____,

I noticed that _____ did really well

in _____ today. Your child showed an amazing

ability to _____

_____

Please congratulate your child on this positive effort!

Sincerely,

_____

0-7682-2608-2 Great Rooms! Grades 2–3

Parent Feedback Form

Dear Parents and Guardians,

I would very much like to hear from you about how the year is going for you and your child. Your child's success is important to me. From your comments, I will be able to evaluate our program and consider changes and improvements that need to be made.

Please take a few moments to provide me with your feedback on the following areas:

Language Arts (Reading/Writing/Spelling) _____

_____

_____

Math _____

_____

Social Studies and Science _____

_____

_____

Homework _____

_____

Classroom Management Plan _____

_____

Please complete the sentences below.

I feel my child has made the most progress in _____

_____

I feel my child has made the least progress in _____

_____

One way you could help my child is by _____

_____

Please write additional comments, questions, or suggestions on the back. Thank you!

Sincerely,

_____

0-7682-2608-2 *Great Rooms! Grades 2–3*

Progress Reports and Report Cards

Student records, such as progress reports and report cards, are best stored in a secure location to protect the privacy of individual students. File these documents in a filing cabinet or a locked drawer for safekeeping when they are not in use.

Progress Reports

Progress reports are used when teachers want to notify parents about student progress midway through the grading period. Typically, a progress report signals parents that their child is having problems in some area of the curriculum. However, many schools and teachers like to send home progress reports that indicate satisfactory progress as well.

Some teachers choose to have students complete a self-evaluation of their progress for these reports. Others simply tally the students' current scores and report those grades to parents. Either way, this is an opportunity to let parents know about the progress of their child before the final grade becomes part of the official school record.

Report Cards

Grades for each student are recorded on report cards and kept on record in the school office. Typically, the report cards are sent home to the students' parents so that they may see the grades in each subject, sign the report card, and return it to the school. Most teachers choose to add comments to document student behavior or academic progress. However, do your best to avoid writing report card comments that will come as a surprise to parents. If you sense that a child is struggling with behavioral or academic issues, contact the parents at the first sign of the problem so that you can meet to discuss ideas and help the student. If the child is still battling the problem at the time that report cards are issued, tactfully document the issue in writing at this time. All students have some area within the school sphere in which they excel. Be sure to give at least one positive statement at the beginning of the comments section.

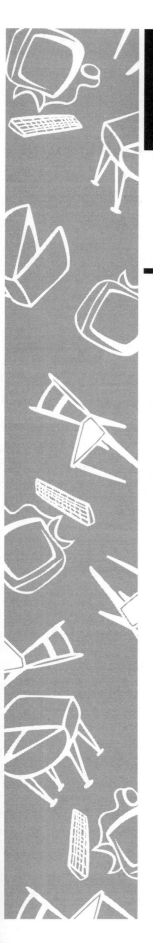

Chapter 5: Learning Centers

Learning centers provide students with the opportunity to work at their own pace in a variety of different activities, either within the scope of the regular curriculum or as an extension of their daily learning.

This chapter includes ideas for:

- learning center setup
- learning center schedules
- learning center rotations
- collecting work
- student accountability
- topic-specific centers

0-7682-2608-2 *Great Rooms! Grades 2–3*

Learning Center Setup

It is not necessary for you to set up your learning centers before the first day of school. Students will need one or two weeks to get acclimated to your classroom and learn your regular daily routine, rules, and procedures before they are ready to work in a learning center setting that requires more self control.

After the first few weeks of school, you may be ready to begin setting up your learning centers in order to reinforce what students are learning in the classroom or to build and extend skills that complement your current curriculum.

Individual Centers

If you have the space in your classroom, set up a table along a wall or in a corner of the room for each learning center. Arrange chairs at each center to accommodate the number of students you want working there at any one time.

Affix a bulletin board or poster board above the learning center table. Post instructions, a folder for papers, and hanging bags for other supplies that are needed for the center activity. In addition, place a cup full of pencils or a bin of crayons or markers on the table for students to use.

At these centers, students will work on the activity, project, or task either as a group or individually. At the close of the center time, have students return the supplies and materials to the appropriate location, clean up the center, and return to their desks.

Temporary Learning Centers

If space does not permit you to arrange permanent learning centers in your classroom, try setting up instant learning centers using folding display boards. These inexpensive, freestanding cardboard displays can be purchased at office supply or craft stores. Best of all, you can decorate the boards, attach folders or pockets with pushpins or staples, and keep them folded and stored in a closet or against the wall until they are ready to be used.

At center time, pull out the displays and stand them up on the floor in various areas of the room. Have a stack of inexpensive folding breakfast trays for students to use as portable desks or writing surfaces as they sit on the floor at each learning center. Or, simply have students use clipboards for writing surfaces as they travel from one center to the next.

Another way to save classroom space while working with learning centers is to set up centers where students simply retrieve materials and get directions for the activity. Students then take the items to their desks where they work on completing the activities. You can even place learning center materials and directions inside small paper gift bags. Hang the bags on coat hooks along a wall for easy storage!

0-7682-2608-2 *Great Rooms! Grades 2–3*

Learning Center Schedules

Scheduling learning center time can be a challenge in any classroom. With so many subjects and curriculum objectives to cover, make the most of your learning centers by tying them to content areas you are already studying. This way, center time is incorporated into your lesson plans, rather than viewed as an "extra" in your classroom.

Five Days a Week

Set aside twenty or thirty minutes each day for learning center time. Create five centers surrounding five different curriculum areas, such as reading, writing, math, social studies, and science. Stock the centers with activities that build upon the concepts you are currently teaching in your classroom. Divide the class into five groups and have the groups rotate through the centers (one center a day for each day of the week) until all groups have completed the activities at each center.

Note: This method requires you to prepare new centers every week, but also allows students to explore independent and cooperative learning through centers more frequently.

One Day a Week

If you have less time to devote to learning center preparations or would like to create a greater variety of learning centers, try setting up a learning center schedule that takes more time for students to complete. Create seven or eight centers surrounding different curriculum areas, such as reading, writing, spelling, listening, math, social studies, science, and art. Divide the class into small learning center groups and have the groups visit one or two centers a week during a weekly hour-long center time. After five to eight weeks, students will have completed the activities at each center. At the end of this rotation, you will need to restructure the activities or change the learning centers so that the activities teach another skill or offer a different challenge.

Learning Center Rotations

In order to make sure each child has a turn at the various learning centers, group students together and have them work through a set rotation in your classroom

Learning Group Chart

Post a Learning Group chart on the wall of your classroom. Assign groups of students to work together at center time. Write the groupings along the left side of the chart. Across the top, list each learning center. The number of groups should be equal to the number of centers. Fill in the chart to show at which center each group should be at day 1, day 2, and so on.

Groups	Reading	Writing	Math	Science	Map	Art
MB, JJ, AW, ZW	1	2	3	4	5	6
KJ, ED, KT, MH	2	3	4	5	6	1
BR, VM, SF, VS	3	4	5	6	1	2
LW, MR, DC, PD	4	5	6	1	2	3
PT, BS, LN, CT	5	6	1	2	3	4
JS, TH, LB, EJ	6	1	2	3	4	5

Learning Group Magnets

Using a marker, write the name of each learning center on a magnet board. Print each student's name on a small magnetic tile. Have students select a center that interests them and place their magnetic tile beneath the name of the corresponding learning center. Set a limit of students per center. Once a center is "full," have students select a different center. After students are placed at their initial center, have them rotate as a group to each center until all have had a turn at the different activities. Be sure to rotate who gets to choose first when you begin a new set of centers.

Learning Group Clothespins

Write each student's name on the side of a clothespin with a marker. Print the names of each learning center around the edges of a sheet of poster board. Assign students to learning centers by clipping each clothespin along the outside of the poster board next to the center's name. When you want children to move to a new learning center, simply rotate their clothespins to a new spot on the poster board.

Collecting Work

Devise a plan for collecting work at the end of each learning center session to help students stay organized and keep track of their work. Here are three methods you may want to consider.

Learning Center Folders

Give each student a pocket folder for storing learning center work. Have students place completed work in the right side of their folders and turn them in to a tray or basket at the end of the session. Once you have checked that their work is completed, put a checkmark or stamp on the papers and return them to the left side of the folders. The next time students work at learning centers, they can remove the papers from the folders and take them home.

Tote Bags

Purchase inexpensive paper tote bags from a party goods store. Give a tote bag to each group. Ask a volunteer in each group to collect completed work, models, projects, or assignments and place them in the group's bag. At the end of each session, have the group volunteers place the bags on your desk.

Baskets

If you have space at each learning center, set up a "completed work" basket. Have students place finished assignments or activities in the basket to be graded later. At the end of the learning center session, ask a materials manager or paper monitor to collect the assignments from each basket around the room.

Student Accountability

Behavior Accountability

Having students work in learning centers often requires that they work together with two or more other students. In order to do this successfully, students will need to have a clear understanding of what is expected of them and other students while working cooperatively in a group. (See sample Learning Center Rules on page 104.) Take some time to set up some class rules that are specific to cooperative learning situations.

Work Accountability

In order to help students stay organized and keep track of their own work, provide each student with a learning center folder. Students can keep incomplete learning center assignments in the folder until they are completed and ready to turn in. You may want to have students store their learning center folders in a central location in the classroom rather than in their individual desks. Label folders with students' names and allow them access to the folders at center time. Have a designated learning center tray, basket, or box in which students can turn in finished assignments.

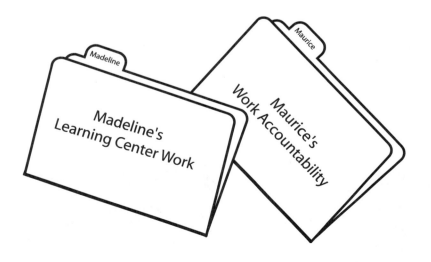

© McGraw-Hill Children's Publishing

0-7682-2608-2 *Great Rooms! Grades 2–3*

Learning Center Rules

1. **Follow directions to complete each task or project.**

2. **Take turns and share learning center materials.**

3. **Be polite to others.**

4. **Use quiet voices.**

5. **Clean up the center when your work is completed.**

0-7682-2608-2 *Great Rooms! Grades 2-3*

Topic-Specific Centers

Reading Center

Having a designated reading center as part of your learning center rotation is an excellent way to promote independent reading. You may want to use the time to encourage students to read books of a particular genre. Introduce them to a genre, such as mysteries, by reading aloud the first chapter of a sample book. Point out other books they might read by the same author, as well as other books in that genre by different authors. If students have a designated time period in which they are required to read silently, they are more likely to be drawn in to the joy of reading.

Make a list of book projects for students to choose from and complete once they have finished their book. Post the list at the center with supplies.

Another approach you might want to take is to utilize the time to meet with small groups of students for a guided reading lesson. Have students sit around a small table with you and take turns reading selections of a story aloud. This will help you monitor each child's reading progress and allow you to make a quick individual assessment of your students' reading abilities. You may also suggest a literature circle approach where several students discuss the same book that they are reading.

Reference Center

Give students opportunities to practice reference skills by setting up a reference center. You can alternate learning activities by using a variety of resources, such as dictionaries, encyclopedias, and thesauruses. Type a list of questions that require students to use the appropriate source to find information or answers, or set up a scavenger-hunt-of-facts, either on a computer with internet access, or in animal encyclopedias or world record almanacs.

More on Centers

Math Center

Using math games and puzzles as enrichment or reinforcement of current math topics is an effective way to engage students in math center activities. The more challenging and fun the game is, the more students are likely to enjoy the activity and forget that they are "doing math." Dice games, card games, logic puzzles, and games involving play money are always a big hit!

Science Center

Set up a science exploration center using simple items such as a microscope, magnifying glass, or magnets. Have students work together to conduct easy experiments, perform demonstrations, or make and record observations. Use this center to extend your science unit or to encourage students to explore additional areas of scientific study.

0-7682-2608-2 *Great Rooms!* Grades 2–3

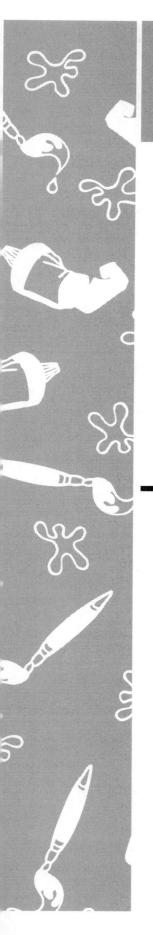

Art Center

Provide children with a creative outlet by setting up an art center. Children enjoy exploring and experimenting with a variety of media, so be sure to change the art activity frequently. For example, one week you may want to have them draw pictures, the next they might paint, and later they could be required to sculpt something out of clay.

Try tying your art center into a current unit of study. For example, if you are reading a play in language arts, have students make stick puppets to represent the characters. If you are studying different Native American tribes, have them make tribal masks or create models of different types of dwellings. If you are exploring geometry in math class, have students make collages with various geometric shapes cut from construction paper.

Here are some items you may want to include in your art center:

- paints and paintbrushes
- markers
- crayons
- pencils
- construction paper
- glue
- fabric scraps
- stapler and staples
- yarn or string

- hole punches
- clay or dough
- waxed paper
- newspaper or newsprint
- googly eyes
- felt pieces
- wooden dowels
- stickers and rubber stamps
- stencils

McGraw-Hill Children's Publishing

0-7682-2608-2 *Great Rooms! Grades 2–3*

World View Center

Invite children to explore the world around them through a geography center. Focus on a certain area of the world by displaying maps of various countries, or challenge students to find different locations on a globe or world map. You can create simple quiz cards on index cards and invite students to divide into teams and challenge each other in a geography game. However you choose to use the center, it's sure to be a hit with your students, while teaching them something new at the same time!

Listening Center

The listening center is always a student favorite. Set up an area where students can use headphones to listen to stories, songs from around the world, or poems and books on tape. You can even use the center to help students improve their listening skills. Simply record a set of instructions on a blank tape. Have students listen carefully to the taped instructions and follow directions, recording their answers or following along with the activity on a sheet of paper. Be sure to set up this center near an electrical outlet for easy access.

0-7682-2608-2 *Great Rooms! Grades 2–*

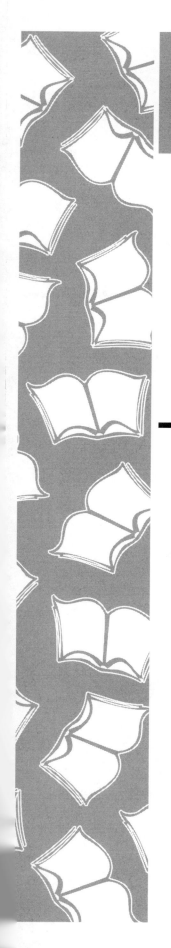

Writing and Publishing Center

Encourage students in creative writing by setting up a writing and publishing center. Provide a variety of publishing supplies, such as paper, rulers, scissors, tape, stapler, pencils, and erasers. It is also helpful to supply students with a special place to store their works in progress. Tape magazine holders or cereal boxes together to create a row of storage containers, and label each one with a student's name. This will allow students to easily find their work each time they visit the writing and publishing center. Be sure to post a list of the steps in the writing process that students can refer to when working at the center.

Creative Book Making

After students have completed the writing process, allow them to have fun with their work. Have students select a type of book to make and turn their final draft into a publication. You may want to reproduce copies of the different book-making directions on pages 110-115 and place them in your publishing center for students to follow.

Bookmarks

Give students bookmarks as reading or book-making incentives. Reproduce the bookmarks on page 116 and have students color in the designs. As they read a certain number of books or write and publish a new book of their own, give students a bookmark reward!

Make a Pop-Up Illustration

You will need these things:

- white copy paper
- construction paper
- crayons or markers

- scissors
- tape
- glue

Instructions:

1. Think about the story you wrote. Choose a scene to illustrate.
   Plan which character or object you want to show as pop-up art.

2. Fold a small strip of paper into fourths.
   Tape the ends together to make a box.

3. Fold a sheet of white copy paper in half. Unfold.
   Draw the background scene on it.

4. Glue the box shape to the inside of the paper at the fold.

5. Color and cut out a pop-up character or object.
   Glue it to the box shape.

6. Fold a sheet of construction paper in half. Glue the scene
   onto the construction paper to frame your pop-up illustration.

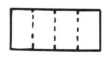  

0-7682-2608-2 *Great Rooms! Grades 2–*

Make a Shape Book

You will need these things:

- 2 sheets of construction paper
- writing paper
- white copy paper
- pencil

- crayons or markers
- scissors
- hole punch
- yarn, string, or metal rings

Instructions:

1. Think about the story you wrote. Choose a shape that matches it.

2. Trace the shape onto both sheets of construction paper to make identical front and back covers. Cut them out.

3. Trace the shape onto sheets of writing paper and copy paper. Cut them out.

4. Copy your story onto the writing paper shapes.
   Draw pictures on the blank paper shapes.

5. Stack the pages and covers. Punch holes at the top of them.
   Tie the pages together with yarn or string, or use metal rings.

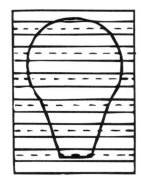

© McGraw-Hill Children's Publishing

0-7682-2608-2 *Great Rooms! Grades 2–3*

Make a Skinny Book

You will need these things:

- 1 sheet of construction paper
- copy paper
- pencil
- crayons or markers
- stapler

Instructions:

1. Fold a few sheets of copy paper in half lengthwise to make pages.

2. Fold the construction paper in half lengthwise to make a cover.

3. Slip the pages into the cover.
   Staple them together along the fold.

4. Write and illustrate a poem or story inside the book.

5. Illustrate and label the cover.

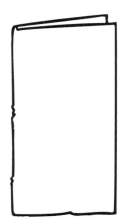  

 0-7682-2608-2 *Great Rooms! Grades 2–*

Make an Accordion Book

You will need these things:

- 11″ x 17″ white paper
- cardstock
- pencil

- crayons or markers
- scissors
- stapler

Instructions:

1. Fold the paper in half lengthwise.

2. Fold the paper back and forth (like an accordion) into an even number of sections.

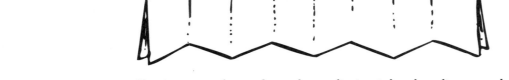

3. Cut two small pieces of cardstock to fit inside the first and last sections.

4. Insert the cardstock into each end and tape the corners.

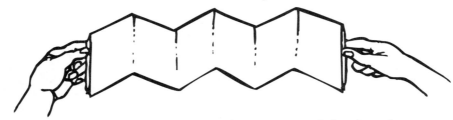

5. Use markers or crayons to decorate the cover of the book.

6. Write a story or poem on the inside pages.

0-7682-2608-2 *Great Rooms! Grades 2–3*

Make a Lift-the-Flap Book

You will need these things:

- paper
- pencil
- scissors
- glue
- crayons or markers
- stapler

Instructions:

1. Write a story about someone or something that is hidden or lost.
2. Design a picture that will hide the person or thing under a flap.
3. Draw and cut out the shape of something in your picture to make a flap.
4. Fold back an edge of your flap shape.
   Glue the edge of the flap to the picture.
5. Open and close the flap.
   Draw the hidden person or thing under the flap.
6. Staple together your story and picture.

0-7682-2608-2 *Great Rooms! Grades 2–3*

Make an Itty-Bitty Book

You will need these things:

- white copy paper
- pencil
- crayons or markers
- scissors

Instructions:

1. Fold the paper in half lengthwise.
   Then fold it in half widthwise two times.
   Unfold it to see eight boxes.

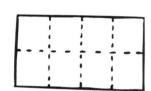

2. Refold the paper in half widthwise.

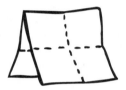

3. Cut halfway down on the middle fold.
   Then unfold the paper again.

4. Fold the paper in half lengthwise.
   Push the ends toward the middle until they meet.

5. Fold the left end toward the right to close the book.

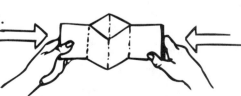

6. Write and illustrate a poem or story in the book.

0-7682-2608-2 *Great Rooms! Grades 2–3*

Bookmarks

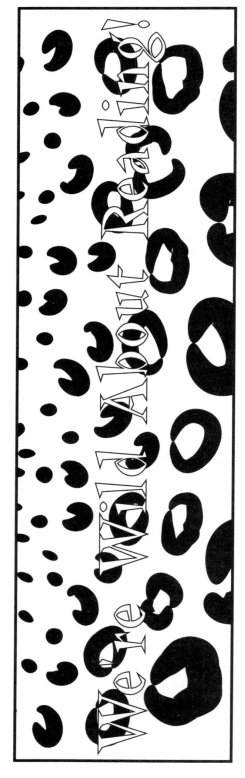

We're Wild About Reading!

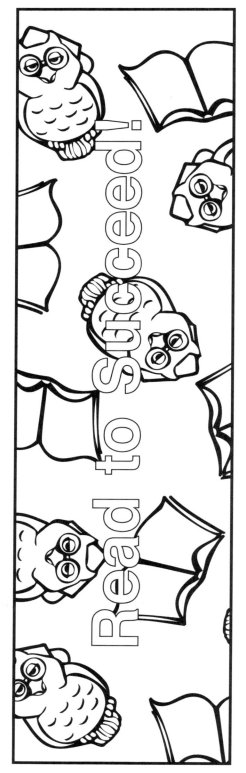

Read to Succeed!

Buddle Up With a Good Book!

0-7682-2608-2 *Great Rooms! Grades 2–3*

Chapter 6: Special Events

An elementary school environment is filled with special events throughout the year! Each event requires different preparations and procedures. From Parents' Night and field trips to classroom parties and school-wide assemblies, this chapter provides tons of ideas for the management and planning of these unique situations.

This chapter includes ideas for:

- Parents' Night
- Open House
- field trips
- parent-teacher conferences
- school assemblies
- classroom celebrations
- special performances
- classroom visitors
- standardized testing

0-7682-2608-2 *Great Rooms! Grades 2–3*

Parents' Night

Parents' Night is an excellent opportunity to meet your students' parents and convey your expectations and plans for the school year. It also provides a chance for parents to learn a little about your background, personality, and teaching style. Because this evening will likely be the first impression that you give to many of the parents, it is important for you to be friendly, organized, confident, and professional. For the most part, parents are looking for reassurance that their child is in the hands of a caring, competent teacher.

Getting Your Room Ready

Of course you will want to make a favorable first impression, so it is important that your room be tidy and appear organized. However, it need not look like a museum showcase. Instead, allow your room to show evidence of student learning and works in progress. Parents of young elementary-school students enjoy seeing their children's schoolwork or artistic creations displayed around the room. Make sure every child has at least one item posted. Enlist students' assistance in preparing the room for their parents' visit. Make copies of the letter frames on page 120. Have students fill in the top portion and leave it on their desk. Encourage parents to write a reply that night on the bottom half of the page.

Sharing Your Background

Before Parents' Night, think about what you would like parents to know about your educational and professional background. Prepare a brief, one- to two-minute monologue or computer slide presentation that outlines your degree (including title, institution, and special teacher training), your experience, and your teaching philosophy. Practice delivering this information to an audience in a natural and professional manner. Remember to smile as you speak and encourage parents to approach you with any specific questions at the close of the presentation.

Outlining Your Curriculum

Give a short overview of the subject matter that you plan to cover throughout the course of the year in each curriculum area. Try to provide parents with examples of the type of work their children will be doing and the level of expectation you have for their abilities. Set up textbooks and sample projects and assignments on tables in the room.

Explaining Your Discipline Plan

During the evening, take a few minutes to explain your discipline plan to parents. Provide parents with a written copy of your classroom rules and expectations for the students. Invite parents to ask questions about your plan and thank them in advance for their cooperation and support.

Parent Questionnaire

Parents want to know that you are interested in the individual needs and interests of their children. Reproduce the questionnaire on page 121 and invite parents to fill it out, either right then or later at home. Explain that the information they provide will help you in gaining a better understanding of the educational needs and goals of each child.

Volunteering in the Classroom

Make a copy of the *Volunteer Interest Form* on page 122. Fill in the blank headings with any volunteer needs you have, such as typing students' stories or assisting with science experiments. Display the sign-up sheet near the door for parents to fill out on Parents' Night. Next, make a copy of the blank calendar on page 124. Fill in the calendar with classroom activities or volunteer opportunities for the current month or an upcoming month. Reproduce a class set to hand out to parents.

Make follow up calls the week after Parents' Night to contact volunteers. Enlist the help of a room parent in making the calls for parents who signed up to help with special events, such as parties and the book fair.

Welcome to Parents' Night!

Dear _____,

Welcome to my classroom!

My teacher's name is _____.

One thing I want you to know about my class is _____

_____

Before you leave tonight, please look at _____

_____

Thank you for coming to meet my teacher and see my classroom!

Your child,

_____

A Friendly Reply!

Dear _____,

_____

_____

_____

_____

Love,

_____

0-7682-2608-2 *Great Rooms! Grades 2–3*

Parent Questionnaire

Your child's name _____

Child's date of birth _____

What is the language primarily spoken in your home? _____

What is your child's favorite subject? _____

_____

In what subject(s) does your child excel? _____

_____

In what subject(s) does your child need improvement? _____

_____

In what extracurricular activities does your child participate? _____

_____

_____

What additional information would you like for me to know about your child? _____

_____

_____

_____

Do you have any questions about the upcoming year? _____

_____

_____

_____

0-7682-2608-2 *Great Rooms! Grades 2–3*

Volunteer Interest Form

Please print your name and phone number. Place a check mark in the boxes beneath the activities that interest you. Either a room parent or I will contact you with volunteer opportunities as they arise. Thank you!

Name _____ Phone number _____

- [ ] Room parent
- [ ] Field trips
- [ ] Class parties
- [ ] Book Fair
- [ ] Arts and crafts
- [ ] Read with individual students
- [ ] Computer assistance for students
- [ ] Filing or photocopying
- [ ] At-home projects

- [ ] I can help on a regular basis.
- [ ] I may be able to help at special events.

0-7682-2608-2 *Great Rooms! Grades 2–3*

Volunteer Request Letter

Dear Parent or Guardian,

We are in need of your help! Your Volunteer Interest Form that we have on file states that you are

interested in helping with _____.

We are in the process of planning a _____

to be held on _____.

Could we count on your help with _____?

Your duties would include:

Please return this request by _____.

Call _____ at

_____ with any questions you may have.

Thank you in advance, for taking an active part in your child's learning environment.

_____   _____

Your Child's Teacher   Date

0-7682-2608-2 *Great Rooms! Grades 2–3*

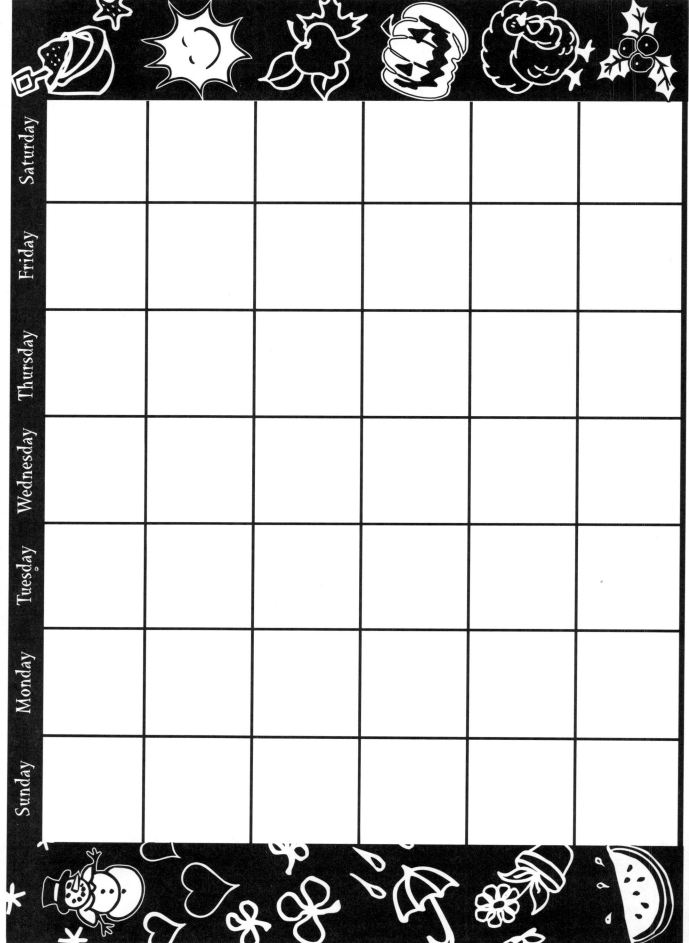

Month of:

Sunday	Monday	Tuesday	Wednesday	Thursday	Friday	Saturday

0-7682-2608-2 *Great Rooms! Grades 2–3*

Open House

Unlike Parents' Night, an Open House generally falls later in the school year. For some schools, it is a culminating event. Open House is an opportunity for parents and other members of the community to tour the school, meet the teachers, and get an overview of what is happening inside the classrooms at your school. Students look forward to attending Open House with their families in order to show off their classroom, introduce their teacher, and share completed projects with loved ones.

Usually, Open House is a casual environment and does not require you to give a group presentation or speech. However, it is a good idea to be prepared to confidently and cheerfully answer questions from current or prospective parents regarding your general teaching philosophy or management style. If parents attempt to involve you in an in-depth discussion of their child's progress, politely offer to meet with them privately at another time that is convenient for them.

Preparing for Open House

Several weeks prior to the scheduled Open House, talk to your class about what they would like to showcase to others. Invite them to reflect over the year and share some of their favorite memories, projects, or things they learned. You may even want to have students select work throughout the year that they would like to put on display during Open House. Have students help you decorate bulletin boards or walls for the occasion.

Open House Video

Use a video camera to create a personalized video of your class for Open House! Give each student a little camera time! Have students introduce themselves and share something they enjoy about school. Parents will enjoy viewing their child and the other students on the small screen. Plus, it will provide them with a little insight into their children's interests at school.

0-7682-2608-2 *Great Rooms! Grades 2–3*

Field Trips

Throughout the year, you may be interested in taking your students on a field trip or educational outing off campus. Before making arrangements for such an adventure, talk to the school secretary or administrators about the school or district guidelines regarding field trips. Make sure you have the necessary paperwork to distribute to parents to sign and return so that every child has permission to accompany you on the journey.

Field Trip Ideas:

- Visit a museum—art, science, natural history, history, children's, etc.
- Go to an aquarium, the zoo, or a wildlife refuge.
- Take a tour of a historic site.
- Go to a beach, forest, garden, or other natural park.
- Attend a concert, dance performance, or play designed for children.
- Visit your local fire department, post office, town hall, or recycling center.
- Visit a downtown library.
- Go to a cultural fair.
- Take a trip to a local farm.
- Visit a senior citizens center.

Steps for Planning a Field Trip

1. Select a field trip site with educational purposes in mind. Preview it.
2. Be able to explain the educational purpose for the field trip as well as its value in enhancing your regular on-site curriculum.
3. Obtain administrative approval for the dates and location of the trip.
4. Secure reservations and bus or carpool transportation.
5. Send home permission slips to be signed by parents or guardians.
6. Recruit chaperones, and give them the information they need.
7. Conduct lessons to prepare for and complement the field trip.

Field Trip Details

Obtaining Administrative Approval

As soon as you identify a prospective field trip destination, make an appointment with your principal or administrator to discuss your plans. Present your principal with an outline of your plans, including date, time, location, number of chaperones, and transportation arrangements. Also, include a brief explanation of the educational value of the field trip so that your administrator will be able to comfortably support your plans.

Securing Reservations

Once you have obtained administrative approval for your trip, you will need to contact the location and finalize your reservations. Here are some questions to ask when inquiring about a possible field trip site or when finalizing reservations:

- *Are there any hidden costs involved?*
- *Is there an area where we can eat lunch? Is lunch included?*
- *Will restrooms be available?*
- *How many chaperones are needed?*
- *Will a first-aid kit be made available?*

- *Is there a required dress code?*
- *Will students need to bring anything?*
- *Do you have any preparatory or follow-up lesson plans available?*
- *Is there a contact person who can meet our bus when we arrive?*

Arranging Transportation

You will probably need to make special transportation arrangements for your class to go on a field trip. Ask the school secretary if there is a procedure for requesting a district school bus or if carpooling is allowed. If parent volunteers will be driving the students in your class, you will need to make a photocopy of their driver's licenses and insurance cards. In addition, you will want to be sure that every car has a working seatbelt for each child who will be riding in it.

Getting Ready

Explain the field trip to your students. Review guidelines for behavior on the bus and at the site. You may want your class to wear matching T-shirts to make the group easily identifiable. Specify a procedure students should follow if they get separated from the group.

Field Trip Follow Up

1. Discuss what the class experienced and learned.
2. Let students create a commemorative project such as a mural or news summary.
3. Write a group or individual 'thank you' letters to each of your field trip helpers.

© McGraw-Hill Children's Publishing 0-7682-2608-2 *Great Rooms! Grades 2–3*

Parent-Teacher Conferences

Parent-teacher conferences provide you with an opportunity to meet with parents to discuss their child's progress in school. To make the experience positive for both parties involved, take time to organize and prepare for each conference. Avoid using scheduled conference times to surprise parents with unexpected concerns. Instead, alert parents at the first sign of concern and use conference times to listen, problem solve, and resolve issues that are already known to parents. Invite parents to share their concerns and questions with you.

Student Progress At-a-Glance

Reproduce a copy of the form on page 129 for each child in your class. Use the form to prepare for parent-teacher conferences. It is not necessary to read from the form during the conference or to supply the form to the parents if you are not comfortable doing so. However, this form will help you to gather and organize your thoughts so that you can clearly present your concerns and comments to parents about their child's progress.

Parent Preparation Letter

Help parents prepare for conferences. Reproduce a copy of the letter on page 130 for each child. Send the letter home to parents along with your own form that indicates the conference times that are available.

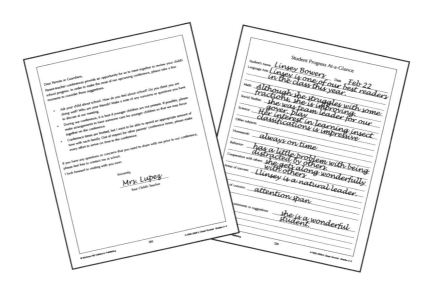

Student Progress At-a-Glance

Student's name _____ Date _____

Language Arts: _____

_____

_____

Math: _____

_____

Social Studies: _____

_____

Science: _____

_____

Other subjects: _____

_____

Homework: _____

_____

Behavior: _____

_____

Cooperation with others: _____

_____

Areas of success: _____

_____

_____

Areas of concern: _____

_____

Additional comments or suggestions _____

_____

_____

0-7682-2608-2 *Great Rooms! Grades 2–3*

Dear Parents or Guardians,

Parent-teacher conferences provide an opportunity for us to meet together to review your child's school progress. In order to make the most of our upcoming conference, please take a few moments to consider these suggestions.

- Ask your child about school: *How do you feel about school? Do you think you are doing well? Who are your friends?* Make a note of any concerns or questions you have to discuss at our meeting.

- During our conference, it is best if younger children are not present. If possible, please make arrangements to have someone care for younger children so that we may focus together on the conference.

- Conference times are limited, but I want to be able to spend an appropriate amount of time with each family. Out of respect for other parents' conference times, please make every effort to arrive on time to the conference.

If you have any questions or concerns that you need to share with me prior to our conference, please feel free to contact me at school.

I look forward to visiting with you soon.

Sincerely,

_____

Your Child's Teacher

0-7682-2608-2 *Great Rooms! Grades 2–3*

School Assemblies

Your school probably has special procedures in place for coordinating and participating in school-wide assemblies. Be sure to ask a fellow teacher or staff member to explain the expectations for attendance, seating arrangements, and general protocol for school assemblies.

For example, here are some questions you might want to ask:

- *Where do school assemblies usually take place?*

- *Are certain grade levels seated in specific sections?*

- *Are teachers expected to sit with their students throughout the assembly?*

- *What is the accepted procedure for handling discipline problems during an assembly?*

- *Does the administration encourage teachers to use the time to correct papers or manage other quiet tasks, or is this frowned upon?*

- *Is there a particular order in which classes are dismissed from school assemblies?*

Once you determine the answers to these questions, take time to educate your students about the procedures and protocols that affect them.

Finally, review your behavior expectations with students and remind them to be attentive and polite during the presentation. Encourage them to show respect for school guests by applauding at the close of the presentation.

0-7682-2608-2 *Great Rooms! Grades 2–3*

Classroom Celebrations

What better way to celebrate classroom successes throughout the year than to throw a party! Whether you are commemorating a national holiday or simply patting your students on the back for a job well done, children love classroom parties! From time to time, set aside your regular school lessons for an afternoon and invite your students to celebrate significant events together.

Events to celebrate:

- Fall Harvest
- Election Day
- winter holidays
- Valentine's Day
- the 100th day of school
- St. Patrick's Day
- School Spirit Day
- summer birthdays
- Music Appreciation Day
- reading success

Involving Parents

When planning a classroom celebration, invite parents to join in the fun! Send home a copy of the letter on page 134. As forms are returned, ask a room parent to organize and coordinate parent volunteers, supplies, and food.

0-7682-2608-2 *Great Rooms! Grades 2–3*

Class Parties

Party Setup

Enlist the help of parent volunteers to help with party setup. While parents are decorating the classroom, take students outside on the playground for a few minutes. This will make decorating much easier and will increase the impact and awe for students as they step into the festively-adorned classroom to enjoy the class party!

Party Behavior

Make students aware of your expectations for their behavior during a class celebration. If you allow students to sit with friends or move their desks together during a party, set a limit to the noise level and review any special rules you have. In addition, take the opportunity to remind students to use good manners when requesting or receiving servings of food and drink from parent volunteers.

Party Cleanup

Do not leave the bulk of your classroom cleanup to parent volunteers. Before the party, explain to students that they will be responsible for depositing their plates, cups, and napkins into trash bags or cans. This will let parents focus on cleaning the serving dishes only and allow them to enjoy the party. Parents will appreciate the extra help that students provide!

Individual Birthday Celebrations

You may want to create a special birthday celebration policy for children whose birthdays fall during the school year. For example, you may decide to allow parents to bring in healthy birthday treats (such as bagels, fruit snacks, or muffins) for the entire class on the student's birthday. Let parents know what time is convenient—morning recess, lunch time, or end of the school day. Have students sing "Happy Birthday" and allow the birthday child to pass out the treats to the class. Fill out the birthday certificate on page 135 in honor of the child's birthday!

We're Having a Party!

Dear Parents or Guardians,

Our class is having a party on _____ from

_____ to _____ to celebrate _____

_____. You are all invited to attend!

In order to make this event a success, we are requesting volunteers to provide

food, drinks, paper goods, and decorations. Please fill out the form below and return it

to the classroom by _____. Thank you!

- -

Parent's name _____   Phone number _____

Child's name _____

_____ I am available to attend the class party.

_____ I will not be able to attend.

_____ I will bring or send this item:

_____ cookies   _____ cupcakes   _____ fruit tray

_____ vegetables   _____ chips & dip   _____ forks/spoons

_____ decorations   _____ cups   _____ plates

_____ drinks   _____ napkins   _____

other (_____)

0-7682-2608-2 *Great Rooms! Grades 2–3*

Happy Birthday,

_____!

Have an INCREDIBLE Day!

_____   _____
Signed   Date

Special Performances

From time to time, you may have special performances in your classroom. Perhaps you are putting on a class play, giving a vocal performance, or inviting students to play instruments in a mini-recital. In any case, you will want to establish procedures for hosting such events. Be sure to invite parents to join in the audience when appropriate.

Classroom Plays

To develop a sense of creativity and an appreciation of theatrical performance, encourage students to put on a play. Choose a familiar story or fairy tale to break into different roles, or have students perform a simple play that is already written. Ask a parent volunteer to help with costumes and scenery. After allowing students time to rehearse, invite parents or students in other classrooms to serve as the audience.

Talent Shows

Invite students to share and appreciate each other's talents by putting on a class talent show. Whether students play musical instruments, sing songs, recite poetry, perform magic tricks, tell jokes, or juggle, encourage all of them to participate. Before the talent show begins, remind students to support one another by clapping appreciatively after each performance.

Share Days

Young students love to show their cherished possessions to others. Set aside a class share day every week or two and invite students to bring one item to share with the class. Ask students to tell what the item is, where they got it, and why they enjoy it. Invite the class to ask the student one or two additional questions about the item. Be sure to make special arrangements for supervision if students want to bring in a pet to share.

0-7682-2608-2 *Great Rooms! Grades 2–3*

Classroom Visitors

Take advantage of the resources in your community by inviting area professionals to visit your classroom. Whether the purpose for the visit is to read a special book, share information about their careers, or educate students about a specific curriculum area, students will enjoy the opportunity to interact with other adults in their community.

Career Day

Invite parents or local community helpers to your classroom for a presentation on different careers. Ask visitors to prepare a two- or three-minute presentation about their jobs and the functions they perform. Encourage students to ask questions of the visitors at the close of the session. Students will enjoy hearing about the different careers.

Read-a-Thon

Schedule a daylong read-a-thon to spark students' interest in reading. Select a supply of fun and entertaining picture books for visitors to share. Ask a variety of different professionals in your community to volunteer fifteen or twenty minutes of their time to read aloud to the students in your class. Encourage them to be animated and theatrical in their readings. Seeing adults model a love of reading will inspire children to give it a try themselves!

Curriculum Connections

If you are studying animals, invite a veterinarian to visit your classroom. If rocks are your focus for science, arrange for a local geologist to talk to your students. Whatever the area of study, enhance your curriculum by bringing in experts from various fields. Not only will this spark students' interest in the subject matter, it also allows them to see a real-world application for the topics they are studying.

0-7682-2608-2 *Great Rooms! Grades 2–3*

Ideas for Classroom Visitors

- Artist
- Auto Mechanic
- Beekeeper
- Chef
- Dentist or dental assistant
- Doctor
- Emergency paramedic
- Firefighter
- Gardener
- Geologist
- Lifeguard

- Mail Carrier
- Pest Control Professional
- Pilot
- Poet
- Police Officer
- Professional sports player
- Radio or television news personality
- SCUBA diver
- Soldier or military officer
- Veterinarian
- Weather Forecaster

Thank Your Guests

After a guest visits your classroom, be sure to have your students write a thank you note! Make copies of page 139, cut them apart, and give each child a letter to complete. Encourage students to identify highlights or key points of the visit that they enjoyed. Collect the letters and put them in an envelope to send to the visitor in appreciation of that person's visit.

0-7682-2608-2 *Great Rooms! Grades 2–3*

Thank You!

Dear _____,

Thank you for visiting our class! It was so kind of you to spend time with us. My favorite

part of your visit was when _____

_____

I learned that_____

_____

Thank you again for being a special class visitor!

Sincerely,

_____

- -

Thank You!

Dear _____,

Thank you for visiting our class! It was so kind of you to spend time with us. My favorite

part of your visit was when _____

_____

I learned that_____

_____

Thank you again for being a special class visitor!

Sincerely,

_____

© McGraw-Hill Children's Publishing

0-7682-2608-2 *Great Rooms! Grades 2–3*

Our Classroom Guests

Date	Visitor	Comments

0-7682-2608-2 *Great Rooms! Grades 2–3*

Standardized Testing

Most school districts designate a time period during the school year to administer standardized tests to students. Often times, school or district funding is determined by school-wide performance on these tests or improvement on performance. For this reason, it is important to make the testing experience as positive as possible for both students and parents.

Practice Tests

Many companies provide practice tests to prepare students for the format of the test. Schedule time to take these practice tests at least a week before the actual test. This will familiarize students with the format, questioning, and language usage they will encounter on their own. In addition, make sure that students understand how to properly mark their answers on their answer sheets.

Easing Concerns

Some students become anxious or nervous during testing. Try to ease students' stress by scheduling fun, relaxing activities, such as working on learning games or puzzles. Or, schedule recess or physical education classes immediately after testing during this week to encourage students to release nervous energy. Encourage students to relax during testing. If they do not know an answer, instruct them to make their best guess and move on. Students need to know that it is okay if they do not know the correct answer, as long as they do their best.

Notifying Parents

Be sure to let parents know in advance that standardized testing is approaching. Reproduce a copy of the parent letter on page 143 to send home with students. This will remind parents of certain guidelines that are helpful to follow during testing periods.

Testing Tips for Students

To make students more comfortable with the test, provide them with the following tips before beginning each section.

- **Reading Comprehension**—Before reading the passage, skim the first one or two questions immediately following the selection. This will give you a purpose for reading and help you to recall the answers more quickly and easily when it is time to answer the questions.

- **Math**—Work the problems on a piece of scratch paper before looking for the answer. Find and mark the same answer on the test. Before marking an answer, ask yourself, "Is this a reasonable answer?"

- **Spelling**—Many of the words on the test may look tricky. Before marking your answer, ask yourself, "Does this word look right?"

Finally, remind students that if they do not know an answer, they should focus on what they do know. Coach them to eliminate silly or unreasonable answers first, and then to make their best guess from the remaining choices.

Testing Conditions

When students are testing, try to make the environment as private and quiet as possible. Allow students plenty of space around their desks. Reproduce the sign on page 144 and post it on the outside of your classroom door. Remember that it is often difficult for young students to sit and concentrate during testing for a long period of time. If possible, try to schedule breaks, or even just a game of Simon Says, between sections of the test.

_____

Date

Dear Parents or Guardians,

Next week we will begin standardized testing in our classroom. In order to ensure that children are prepared to do their best, please consider following these guidelines:

- Make sure your child goes to bed early and gets a restful night's sleep.

- Encourage your child to eat a healthy breakfast in the morning.

- Please make sure your child arrives to school early or on time.

- If possible, avoid scheduling doctor or dentist's appointments during school hours the week of testing.

- Talk to your child about the importance of doing his or her best on the test. Try to answer your child's questions and ease anxiety about test taking.

Thank you in advance for your support.

Sincerely,

_____

Your Child's Teacher

QUIET PLEASE! STUDENT TESTING IN PROGRESS

0-7682-2608-2 *Great Rooms! Grades 2–3*